ENDOI

"If you have aspirations of becoming an exceptional athlete some-day, would you seek the mentoring of a guy who almost quit sports completely after the 5th grade because he had hurt too many people? Someone who had suffered a broken leg, a broken back, a near-fatal car wreck, and was once wrongly accused of attempted murder? One who showed the signs of excellence in three sports, but never reached his potential due to wild adversities? I would. Because this describes a guy who has been to the house of suffering multiple times in his life, in a wide variety of contexts, and has recognized the sovereign and loving hand of God working to outfit him — not ONLY for the athletic world, but for eternity. And if I could choose, HE'S the guy I would want to lead me, because he does not speak theoretically. He speaks from the reality of the crucible of affliction and can pass on the strength he has gained through what he has written. Michael shares his stories and his insights in a way that will make you remember and make you grow."

—Chris Adsit,
Author of *Personal Disciple-making*,
1975 USA decathlon team

"This book will encourage your faith and point you to God, the One who can help you through life's hardest trials. Many athletes find their identity in sport, and injuries can cause them to become angry, depressed, or even question their purpose in life. Mike's story reminds us that God can bring amazing blessings from our hardest moments in life."

—Leah Amico,
3-time Olympic Gold medalist,
USA Softball

"Mike's book is the real deal when it comes to winning the game of life God invites us into through Jesus. His story of setbacks and failures along the way is so encouraging."

—Brad Barshaw, pastor,
mentor, and friend

"This is a story of God's faithfulness and willingness to love us through whatever trials we may go through. I learn more about my heavenly and earthly fathers every time I open up this book, and the *More Than That* truth is one I will be sharing with my own kids one day."

—Christopher Kalia Buchanan,
son, who brings me great joy!

"After recently coming off a knee surgery myself, reading through Mike's book brought me encouragement and wisdom confirming God's active role in my life and its setbacks. His story of challenges and triumphs is a must-read that offers great insight into the ever-present faithfulness of God."

—Micah Christenson,
USA Olympic Volleyball (Bronze medalist),
USC volleyball captain and 3-time All-American,
AIA student leader

More Than That shares Mike Buchanan's tumultuous journey through life and how he slowly let God strip away his pride through athletic injuries. One at a time, sport by sport, Mike relinquished his idols and replaced them with God's truth and grace. Mike transparently delivers an account of his journey, illustrating how God refined his character and then reflected God's light onto the many he has influenced through a life of service."

—Janice Harrer, Hall of Fame
Professional Beach Volleyball player,
University of Oregon Beach Volleyball coach

"This book is a very fun read. Mike isn't writing about the theoretical, but about an actual lifelong walk with Jesus and some of the big Ebenezers, stones of remembrance, that show how faithful the Lord has been, is, and continues to be. It's a refreshing book and reminds us all that our stories look the same. A lot of daily, faithful obedience mixed in with a few large portraits of the Lord's grace in our lives."

—Ryan Hollingshead, MLS FC Dallas,
UCLA captain and All-American, AIA
student leader

"For over 20 years, I have greatly admired Mike Buchanan's authentic and steadfast walk with the Lord. His life story is very compelling, and I believe it will challenge, encourage, and impact your heart. My hope is that you will walk away from your time reading more inspired and drawn toward the God who has so faithfully sustained Mike throughout the various trials he has endured in his life."

—Kevin Jordan, friend, and ministry
partner at UCLA, played at UCLA
and in the NFL, and served as an NFL Chaplain
for the Steelers, founded 4TheJourney ministry

"My long-time friend and warrior brother, Mike, has written a long overdue book on a subject that has affected millions of us. I commend his work and recommend to all who rely on the physical body to accomplish the mission of the individual as well as the team."

—Victor Marx, Founder and President of
All Things Possible Ministries, 7th degree black belt

"I've had the privilege of being mentored by Mike and have been constantly encouraged by the transparency of his life and his zeal for the Lord. *More Than That* gives a glimpse into his walk with the Lord through his real stories and setbacks. His lessons are relatable and authentic, which makes this a must-read!"

—Nick Valaika, a treasured disciple,
minor leaguer Pittsburgh Pirates,
UCLA baseball captain, AIA student leader

"Reading this book took me down a path of remembrance of my career path as an athlete. The decision to let God take the wheel or ridicule His decision. James 1:2–4 is what I came back to as well to get me through those trials. Mr. Buchanan elegantly puts the life of an athlete in this book, and I believe it is a must-read!"

—Alteraun Verner
NFL Pro Bowler Titans, Bucks & Dolphins,
UCLA All-American, AIA student leader

"God whispers to us in our pleasures ... but shouts in our pains." —C.S. Lewis

MORE

THAN THAT

Biblical Principles for Dealing with Athletic Injuries

written by
Mike Buchanan,
S.D.G.

MORE THAN THAT
Copyright © 2019 by Mike Buchanan, S.D.G.

ISBN: 9781072126126

Cover Design: Alex Pico
Cover Image: Johnny Buchanan
Cover Photographer: Mike Buchanan
Interior Design: Katie Brady
Editor: Tricia Bennett

Printed in the United States of America

ACKNOWLEDGMENTS

After a restless night of prayer, I felt the Lord leading me to write this book. But I thought, *I am not a writer. No way!* The Lord has a sense of humor. The very next day I was blessed to have Dr. Bill Bright, founder of Cru (formerly Campus Crusade for Christ), on my radio show. I had a surprise for him and his wife, Vonette, who was not able to come due to a health issue. I brought a student-athlete, Chris Shinnick, to co-host with me that day. I did not tell Dr. Bright the student's last name when I introduced him because that would have given the surprise away. On the ride to the radio station, Dr. Bright asked me to share my story with him. I shared what is in this book. At the radio station he pulled me aside and said, "Mike, you have got to write your story in book form. I will endorse it for you and help you publish it." (Sadly, that is too late now, as Dr. Bright passed away in 2003.) Through his unsolicited words, Bill Bright confirmed my thoughts from the previous night's wrestling match with the Lord. Therefore, my first thank you goes to Bill Bright, one of the most humble men I have ever had the pleasure of meeting.

My surprise for Bill and Vonette was having Chris's parents call into the radio show after a couple of minutes; they were two of Bill and Vonette's first converts at UCLA where they started Campus Crusade for Christ. Bill's eyes welled up with joy as he talked to Don and Marsha Shinnick after many years. Then Chris chimed in and said, "Hi, Mom and Dad!" The look on Bill's face was indescribable. Dr. Bright was so blessed by that interaction.

Still, I was not sold with the Lord's confirmation. Over the next year while speaking at churches on Oahu, I asked God to confirm that this book idea was truly from Him. I had no faith in my ability to write a book. After I spoke at a church, a young teenage boy came up and said, "Mr. Buchanan, you need to write a book and tell your story." Again, totally unsolicited.

Not long after that, I did my brother-in-law's funeral in California. A lady came up to me and said, "Forgive me, but I feel God wants me to tell you to do what He has revealed to you to do!" Then she asked, "What is it He is calling you to do?" I told her about the book. She teared up and said, "You must do it! Write your book. My two brothers both played in the NFL, and both had career-ending injuries. Their bitterness has kept them from Jesus." I knew the two players she was talking about when she told me her last name.

Yet again, after preaching at another church on Oahu, my son Chris's kindergarten teacher hugged me and said simply, "Mike, you need to write your story." I told her she was the fourth person to confirm this assignment in the past nine months. Thank you, Mrs. Kaneshiro.

Over the past 15 years, every time I go out to spend time alone with God, I start by asking Him, "God, what do I need to confess?" And each time, this book comes to mind first. Obviously I am a slow learner.

I would like to thank my parents and in-laws for being such a great support system and for their unconditional love. And thank you to my greatest cheerleader, Alison, my best friend and my bride, and my daughter, Emily, who both have helped me write this book through reading, critiquing, and adding corrections and thoughts they have shared! To my oldest son, Chris, for reading and endorsing this book, and finally to Johnny, my youngest son, who is an overcomer, who has a story already worthy of a book ... thank you! Johnny is on the cover juggling the balls for me because he looks like I did as a teenager.

I am also grateful to Carolyn Yeargan, who has been praying for me since I was a preteen, my angel of prayer. I think of people who prayed for me and encouraged me greatly: my uncle Rick Wonders, Bill Martz, Kenny Knight, Gary Proud, and so many more who surrounded me in my youth. To my spiritual heroes: Scott Ardavanis, Mike Bunkley, Brad Barshaw, and my father, Keith Buchanan. Thank you with the deepest appreciation for letting Jesus use you to form me into the man I've become. To the boys I ran with in high school and college and to men like Victor Marx and Chris Adsit who are my kindred spirits on this journey of faith, thank you all for being great examples. Finally, a special thanks goes to John Buoncristiani, who has been by my side for four decades, walking with me through all the personal stories in this book as a true friend since the day we met in high school. I am grateful that John has generously written the Foreword to this book. I love you all!

TABLE OF CONTENTS

FOREWORD

"The sculpture is already complete within the marble block, before I start my work. It is already there, I just have to chisel away the superfluous material."

—MICHELANGELO BUONARROTI, FAMOUS SCULPTOR,
ARTIST, AND ARCHITECT

Having no artistic talent myself, I have always been amazed at how artists can create such beautiful things from almost nothing at all. Even though Michelangelo has received resounding and long-standing accolades for his works, this truly pales in comparison to the work that God does in each and every one of our lives on a daily basis. Sculpting marble is a tenuous and painstaking process. Each piece that is chipped away releases more and more of the beautiful creation underneath. Unfortunately, for us it is not just cold marble and stone getting chipped and sanded, but rather flesh, pain, emotions, pride, and tears.

Creating God's beautiful, complete, and good work in our lives is a complicated process, a difficult and painful one as well. While I know that God doesn't take any pleasure in our pain, I am reassured that His work brings about His greater glory and my greatest good. There is no greater craftsman, none wiser or more skilled. We may struggle to imagine what God sees in us sometimes, but it gives me great hope to know that God already sees a complete work in me from the very beginning. God sees greatness and usefulness in all of us. We each have an important role to play in completing His perfect will, not only in our own lives, but also in the lives of those around us.

It is of deep reassurance to me that often it is in the midst of, and sometimes even through, our own greatest failures and pain that God shows up and does His greatest and most glorious work. We can be confident of this not only at our high points, but even more so in the midst of our lowest and seemingly hopeless situations. As God sculpts and carves chunks of "marble" out of our lives, we more closely resemble who we are to become, and the greatness of our Lord becomes even more clear.

I have been privileged to be a part of Mike's life through many of our formative years. Like you, we have both been through a lot of God's reconstructive sculpting! Mike's book illustrates with detail some of the amazing things that God has done in his life. This process is obviously going to look different for each one of us. Painful as it may have been and often how it may continue to be, we are all under the sculpting and construction process that our Lord and Maker has determined for our lives. Sometimes our decisions make this process more painful than it needs to be. Sometimes our process is made more difficult simply because others made poor decisions. But we can rest assured that this process of sculpting a beautiful creation is already complete in God's eye, even before it has begun. Removing the superfluous things from our life is rarely a comfortable undertaking, and each of us faces a different set of circumstances and tools as we undergo our transformation. Some of us take a much longer and more dramatic process than others. But ALL of us have a beautiful and complete sculpture inside of us, waiting to be revealed in God's perfect time. I know you will enjoy reading about the path that God chose for Mike's life.

John Buoncristiani

INTRODUCTION

"Pain insists upon being attended to. God whispers to us in our pleasures, speaks in our consciences, but shouts in our pains. It is his megaphone to rouse a deaf world."

—C.S. Lewis

Athletes take risks every time they show up to compete — common are pulled hamstrings, broken legs, concussions, and even broken necks and death happen. I have experienced my own share of hardships and have been an eyewitness to many more. Over the course of my life, I have faced discouragement, my identity has been lost, my dreams have been shattered, and I have been left wondering, "What's left?" I have learned that although it may not feel like it, God is in absolute control; nothing surprises Him. He loves us *More Than That*.

The title of this book — *More Than That* — came to me as I played with my children, Chris, Emily, and Johnny. At some point when they were between the ages of 4 and 5, I would play this game with each one. I would stretch out my arms and ask, "Does Daddy love you this much?" and each would respond "Yes!" But I would say, "No, I love you more than that!" Then they would expand on the thought, growing from here to the moon, and I would say, "Nope, more than that!" And the game continued on and on like that. As each one of my children reached about the age of 5, they would ask, "Do you love me more than God does?" I would have to answer, "No, God loves you more than I do." That, my friend, is the point of this book — whatever you have suffered in life, God loves you *More Than That.*

As you read my story of redemption, understand that each step along the journey had the design of molding me as a follower of God, a journey that I continue to pursue and endure. I did not choose this journey, but God chose it for me by pursuing me and not letting me stay where I was. He used both my injuries and those hurts I caused to turn my eyes toward Him. He used people in the midst of my trials to direct me toward Him. I encourage you to see God, not me, as you read my testimony, for it is ultimately His story.

PART ONE:
HOW MY JOURNEY STARTED

Chapter 1

SCARED THE "HELL" OUT OF ME

After a broken nose, a shattered kneecap, and a broken neck, I was aware by 5th grade that I was not a good person. None of those things happened to me; rather, I was the cause of them all.

After I had received a stern warning by a teacher, Ms. Tucker, not to throw the dodgeballs at people from one court to the other, a ball happened to roll over to me from another court. Disobeying the teacher, I whipped the ball at an older girl thinking to myself, *Throw it at her knees so she doesn't get hurt.* But just after I threw the ball, the girl dropped to her hands and knees, and the ball hit her square on the nose, breaking it. That teacher confronted me saying, "You'd better pray to God you do not have me as a teacher next year!" Well, I got her. (This particular teacher taught the basics, and she also preached at us all the time not to be prejudiced and to learn from others' differences. She impacted my life with her message of oneness. Thank you!)

The next year, as I was pitching in a baseball game, I encountered a good friend in the batter's box. Richie had moved away but was still playing at the same Little League. He was voted by our class as being the most fair on the playground, and after that honor, Ms. Tucker had asked Richie who he thought was the most fair on the playground. He replied, "Mike," which made me feel great. So as he stepped into the batter's box, Richie and I exchanged smiles. Then I wound up and threw a fastball inside, too far inside. Richie turned his body, and the ball hit squarely on his kneecap, shattering it. I never saw or heard from him again after that incident.

In 5th grade, I also played tackle football for the first time. I was taller than everyone on my team, the Northridge Knights. One day we were playing against the other Northridge Knights team (producing a rivalry for bragging rights at school). With just a few seconds left in the game, my team had just scored to take the lead. There was only time left for a kickoff return. My coach pulled me aside and told me to wait at the 50-yard line in case the other team's runner got loose. The ball was kicked off. From my view, I saw a clump of 21 boys in uniform.

Then Keith, a kid on the other team, emerged with the ball and two blockers, running past everyone. He wisely got behind his two blockers who were shoulder to shoulder. They probably thought they had won the game; the fans' enthusiasm changed dramatically from one side of the field to the other, and it was up to me. They had 10 yards on those chasing them. I knew not to stand flat-footed or I would get decked, so I sprinted at this tight triangle, hitting the two blockers with everything I had. Keith then jumped out to his right. Keeping my eyes up, I saw his move and threw out my long, lanky arm, catching Keith right below the face mask. I had just clotheslined him. Inside I was thinking, *YES! I saved the game!* With Keith's momentum, his feet went straight up and he was now doing a gainer of sorts, but he was not tucked. As he came down and landed on his face mask, I started celebrating our team's win. I thought the reason why Keith was staying on the ground was because he was bummed. Immediately his coaches and the medical team and then the ambulance came on the field. In that moment, my heart sank. Later on I heard that Keith had fractured his neck. I felt horrible and thought to myself, *He could have been paralyzed or even died. I have hurt too many people by the age of 11.*

The next day my family went to a Sunday night church service. There was a guest speaker whose talk was about heaven and hell. I thought that if anyone deserved to go to hell, it was me. I went home that night and begged God in my prayers to save me. I remember my pillow being saturated in tears because this guy's talk on heaven and hell "scared the hell out of me." So I took out fire insurance that night in my prayers for salvation.

Chapter 2

TORMENTED

My time at Robert Frost Junior High School ushered in three of the most miserable, insecure years of my life. Acne blossomed, and my uncles would tease me mercilessly. They would say things like, "Hey, we invited a blind girl over to see if she could read your face for a prophetic message." I also had oily hair and was skinny so they would say, "Hey, when you go to take a shower, do you need to put pencils in your ears so you don't go down the drain?" "Hey, turn sideways, Mike, and stick out your tongue. See, he looks like a zipper." In less than six months, I grew about seven inches, which caused me to have painful cramps, loss of coordination because my arms got long, and trouble catching a ball.

My troubles continued: I had no one to talk to, I sat alone on the bus, and girls did not even want to look at me. Understandably, I had a horrible self-image. I went to youth group regularly because there I felt accepted, but that acceptance came from a group of guys who were not the best influences. The group of us started ditching church frequently and going to Van Nuys Blvd., where the cars cruised at night. Out of that group of friends, all were having troubles "with the law." And in high school they got asked to leave the Christian high school where I was hoping to go.

By the grace of God, a family friend's daughter, Diane, came up to me when I was attempting to ditch church. She grabbed me by the hand and said, "Don't go with them; stay here." I made the right choice that day and continued going to church. For the first time, I felt accepted by the right people, and the youth group became my safe haven. I began feeling God's love in new ways through people. Another way I experienced God's love for me was through a lady named Carolyn Yeargan. I know that Carolyn was praying for me through my junior high and high school years and continues to do so, even to this day. Through these many years, this godly woman has consistently checked in with me. I love her for that.

During this time, I was one person at church and another at school. At school, because I did not want to hurt anybody else after my 5th-grade experiences, I would do nothing when kids tormented me as they tried to find the pecking order in the boys' world. Several kids learning karate, Keith and Steve, would find me on the handball courts and practice their kicks on me. And when guys were being initiated into gangs, they would be dared to come after me, the tall guy. They tried to start fights by hitting me in the face or kicking me, but I would do nothing. My elementary school friend, Jeff, would tell me to stand up for myself. Another friend named Peter, who would become a starting fullback in high school and who was a boy in a man's body even in junior high, would tell me I needed to show some backbone. Honestly, I was afraid of myself because I knew if I got out of control, I could hurt someone. I was that tightly wound. In my mind it was better for me to just feel the physical and emotional pain of being tormented rather than take that chance.

Meanwhile, Los Angeles Unified School District started busing students from the inner city out to my school in the suburbs. The media were around every Tuesday ready to cover the conflicts that might arise. Remembering Ms. Tucker's words regarding equality, I made a couple of friends with the new students. One of my new friends asked me one day if he could hit me after school. I thought, *What?* He went on to explain. Apparently, the guys on the bus had told him that if he did not hit "a white guy" that day, then he would get beat up by a gang of boys who rode on his bus. After school that day as I was walking to the bus, he ran up from the side, hit me, and said, "Thanks, Mike, see ya tomorrow." In that moment, I felt like I was protecting a friend.

Later that year, I was asked to play in the PE class softball All-Star game. *Cool!* I thought. Truthfully, coaches saw a little something in me. We had a test back then to see how far you could throw a softball; I threw it over 280 feet, which would have been a school record if I could have stayed after school on the day when students were vying for records.

When I swung a baseball bat, because I was long and lanky, I stepped away from the plate with my front foot. This would cause me to hit the backstop on my follow through. Everyone seemed to get a laugh at my expense. So during this All-Star game, even though the bell rang, the bases were loaded, and everyone shouted for one more pitch. I was up. I was thinking that I could win the game if I crushed it. I assumed, in my insecurities, that those watching wanted to see the big dork hit the backstop. The pitch came; I swung and nailed it. I saw the ball going over the future All-American shortstop's head. *I would be the hero!* I thought. Then the follow through of my swing made a different sound. I had unknowingly hit Kevin across the head! He had already left another diamond where other teams were playing and was running to the locker room. My bat had opened him up and dropped him on the blacktop. Kevin was a friend in junior high, and he happened to be black, but he was not from the inner city where the kids were bused in from. I was scared now! Coach Means took me into his office and yelled at me, "If that were my son, I would sue you and your parents for everything they have." I wonder if he reacted that way because he was supposed to be the one supervising us.

I never told my parents about this incident until decades later. It scared me, and I lived with the fear of having ruined our family's life. But it also forced me to church, and I grabbed onto God's lapels and held on. It was His and my secret. In retrospect, I see that this was another step in my process of trusting Jesus as my Lord and Savior. I needed Him more than ever.

I continued to incur injury and embarrassing moments during junior high. Another incident occurred when my classmates and I were doing gymnastics testing. I was comfortable doing a handspring off the pommel horse and landing it well. While the teacher was testing us, I started my approach, but someone purposely bumped me on my way to the springboard. As a result, I kicked the front of it, which caused me to trip so that my pelvis hit the front side of the horse. This doubled me up and flung me around where my face came up under the horse on the other side. One of those big bolts punctured right between my eyes at eyebrow level, splitting me open. The teacher got mad at me like it was my fault, and again, I was laughed at. The only person who showed compassion was a really cute girl named Tracy, who got paper towels for me and put her arm around me until I stopped bleeding.

Finally, in 9th grade, I was so excited to play in an after-school basketball league. The All-Star game was played in front of the whole school. My excitement stemmed from the fact that I was the only one playing in the game who could get rim at this age and grade. I was hoping and praying for a breakaway to show off my hops in front of the whole school. I thought that perhaps with the extra adrenaline, maybe I could even dunk. Within the last minute of the game, I got my breakaway. I spotted the rim and headed for it. Having just stepped inside the free-throw line, I was planting my left foot on the next big bounding step, with the buzzer ready to go off, and I was up like Superman. Then I was suddenly shooting like a speeding bullet, catapulted face first to the ground because an opposing player grabbed my shorts on takeoff and pulled them down around my knees. Ball in hands, straight-on face plant, I was completely prostrate on the ground with my shorts down past my knees. The absolute worst part was that day was the first time I wore a jockstrap to play in the big game; I was imitating my dad, because he was my hero. But there, in front of the whole school and for all to see, was my bare butt framed by a Bike jockstrap. Quickly I pulled up my shorts, with my face as red as Rudolph's nose, and literally crawled to the locker room in embarrassment. The roar of all those students laughing at me was painful and mortifying.

During this part of my growing up, these events were humiliating, shameful, and deeply discouraging. However, God continued to hold my life.

Chapter 3
AN IDENTITY FOUND

Going into high school, I had such a poor self-image that part of me hoped I could make a sports team but another part feared failure, even though all my junior high PE coaches told me that they thought I would be good in high school sports. Additional support came from some friends, Coach Tamburo and Coach York, who believed in me more than I believed in myself, but they were already established high school and college coaches. My dad was very encouraging as well; he told me, "You must be committed so only do it if you love it and can give 100%."

I'd like to say I headed to Granada Hills High School for summer school full of confidence, but that would be far from the truth. In actuality, fear was my predominant emotion, but I had some moments in which I experienced a trace amount of hope. I needed a class I had to take to get into L.A. Baptist High School. I also took a football class for incoming students.

Coach Darrel Stroah, a military drill instructor, was in charge of that football class. Dropping a pass meant a bear crawl for 100 yards before getting back in line. I rarely dropped a pass. So Coach Stroah noticed me, and then he tried me at quarterback. I did not think I was smart enough to play there, but during the first two weeks I emerged as one of the top two incoming athletes in that class. The previous year's three-sport star was coming during week three of summer school to work out with us underclassmen. Rumors flew, with comments like "Do not expect him to give you the time of day" and "He will yell at you." All we knew was that his name was John.

John was a punter, and soon I started punting with him almost daily. Suddenly, I was the only quarterback who could throw the ball adequately enough back and forth with him. I became his workout partner; I was giving it all I had just to warm up with him. From John I learned to catch properly, getting my hands out in front so I didn't get dotted on the chest (or wherever the ball hit), leaving a mark, if not a bruise. One day I saw him take a guy off his feet with a heavy ball on a curl route.

After class, John always had me on his basketball team to rebound for him so he could shoot; he called me Wilt. Because of his status as an athlete, he gave me access to the gym floor and a shorter wait to play. Then we would go to the blacktop to throw the baseball. He had this bat that had a net on the end of it about 6 inches long and 3 inches wide. I would throw tennis balls and the net was where the sweet spot of the bat was. We did this for a couple of hours a day, every day for three to four weeks.

Coach Stroah told John that I was transferring to a private school. They both wanted me to stay and play ball at Granada Hills. John came up to me and said, "Coach told me you're transferring. Is that true?" "Yep," I answered. Then John said, "Coach wants me to talk you into staying, and I want you to know I see myself in you." That warmed my soul to hear those words from John at a time when I lacked so much confidence; in fact, his words breathed a new confidence into me.

What's funny is that John's dad was a college football coach. John told me his dad thought his best sport at that point was basketball. John ended up going to Stanford and played both baseball and football. He went on to play both sports professionally and is a Hall of Fame football player from the Denver Broncos — John Elway.

John influenced and encouraged me at a time when I needed it. Much later, I was blessed to serve at the Pro Bowl game in Honolulu, and I ran into John. Even though he did not remember me, John made a major impact on my life.

PART TWO:
THREE LIFE-CHANGING PRAYERS

Chapter 4

"BREAK HIS LEG": MY FOOTBALL STORY

It was my senior year in high school, and the week leading up to Saturday, October 20, 1979, for a football game against Whittier Christian High School on L.A. Baptist's home field. Let me describe what that week, leading up to that big game, looked like for me. First, I was encouraged by our Athletic Director, Dr. Ivan Mears (Doc), that all my coaches had told him they had great expectations for me my senior year. Doc told me he believed I could be All-CIF in all three sports; that would be a first in our small school's history. Doc Mears was my Barnabas (encourager) from junior high through high school.

In spite of these encouraging words about my athletic abilities, I was in a bad place spiritually and emotionally. My thinking was that I had been giving so much of myself to others the previous school year yet little care was reciprocated back to me. So my attitude became: "Screw all those friends at school and church that I've invested in. It's time to take care of myself, make my own way." That thinking was a slippery slope for me. My attitude was bad and self-centered, and my mouth followed. I was no longer caring and encouraging.

It had come to the point where, early in that week, a close

friend of mine, Kathy, came up to me and said, "Mike, your mouth is getting so bad, people are not going to want to hang out with you. That includes me." I respected Kathy so much, and her words crushed me; I went from 6'4" to about an inch tall in that moment. That was at recess. Then at lunch, another caring friend, Mark, came up to me and almost verbatim said the exact same thing. Two people whom I respected cared enough about me to tell me the truth. Yet I heard, "You are being a jerk, Mike." I was crushed like an aluminum can.

Then on Thursday of that same week, I was called out of Spanish class by a counselor on campus whom I had never met before, Miss Britton. *What now?* I thought. She was an ex-cheerleader from our school, now a guidance counselor. I walked into this petite lady's office and asked her why she had called me out of class. She told me she wanted to talk and share an observation with me. In a kind voice, she told me that the previous school year, she had seen me as a spiritual light on campus, but that this year she had not seen that in me. If only I would have had the humility to say thank you that she cared enough to tell me the truth. Instead, I stood right up and said in anger and defensiveness, "You took me out of class to tell me this?" I proceeded to slam my fist into the top of her desk (I am sure others heard it) and said, "Who in the hell do you think you are!" She shocked me when she popped right up from her chair and leaned toward me saying, "Mike, someone had to tell me my senior year, too."

In spite of my outward anger, inside I felt like someone had just put their foot down on this aluminum can and then kicked it. What I couldn't see was that God was using Kathy, Mark, and Miss Britton that week.

On Friday, Athletic Director Ivan Mears told me that he had been contacted by some friends whom he had played with at UCLA. These friends were Terry Donahue's scouts from UCLA, and they were coming to the game to look at me, a couple of my teammates, and several of Whittier's players too. Wow! I felt excited, thinking that Dr. Mears believed in me more than I did myself. After practice that Friday, our coach named the team captains, and I was one of them for the next day's game. That season, I was number one or two in CIF in punting with a 46-yard average, and I was on my way to being chosen All-League at my defensive and offensive positions.

That afternoon I went home. It was typical for my younger brothers to stay clear of me the night before a football game. Unfortunately, I don't know what I did or said to my mom after school, but she told me that she would NOT be coming to the game the next day because she was so upset with me. I usually got in game mode way too early. I decided to stay home that night and focus, getting ready for the game. As I laid in bed, I thought about the words spoken to me that week from Kathy, Mark, and Miss Britton; I begged God to forgive me. I started thinking how I might be a spiritual light on campus once again, being a friend to those I had shoved away. So I came up with a plan. I happened to know four or five of the Whittier players from previous competitions and summer camps, and I realized they might respond to my leading. So I thought and prayed, *Lord, why don't You take someone like _____ (inserting the name during my prayer of one of my teammates), who is not that good of a football player (but a great person), and break his leg. I will then get both teams together and lead a prayer, and start being Your spiritual light on campus again.* Yes, I actually prayed this as I wrestled with the Lord in my bed trying to sleep.

Saturday. Game Day. I was my usual self. Before a game, I typically walked around with a little 18" Dodger bat hitting my body, getting pumped for the game. *Today is going to be a great day!* I thought. When I got to school, I saw Dr. Mears on the way out to the field. "They're here," he whispered to me as I walked by, referring to the UCLA scouts.

The game got under way. I remember Whittier's team trying to use a misdirection play and pitch to their All-CIF running back toward my direction; I was waiting three yards in their backfield for him. As he tried to turn the corner, John, known as "Cap," put his hand down as he was slipping going full speed trying to get away from me. I could have let his knee touch, but I had a great angle. We met helmet to helmet, and he went sliding back about three yards. Cap jumped up and said, "I knew that was you, Buck" (using my nickname). Another play occurred where I was to punt, but there was a penalty. I was aware that the scouts wanted to see me punt because I had a 46-yard average at this point in the season. Darn it. Whittier scored with a minute to go before halftime. So it's time for kickoff return.

The player whom I had named in my prayer the night before came onto the field to take my spot. I ran to our coach and said, "Coach, really?" He responded, "He has not played all year; you get a breather." I retorted, "Coach, I got 20 minutes coming in a minute." Without hesitation and without permission, I turned and sent that player off the field to the bench and waited for the kickoff.

My teammate Mark was deep, and I was one level in front of him as the ball was kicked off. Mark received the ball and went up the left sideline, while I ran to get in front of him. Yet the play went awry. At about the 25-yard line, I led Mark into a bunch of red and white Whittier uniforms. I planted my right foot, Mark went down behind me, the whistle blew, and I looked up just in time to see the biggest guy in our league, who was on the opposing team. At that fateful moment, his head led him forward and found my exposed shin, and the force of his helmet snapped through my tibia and fibula.

At that exact moment, my uncle Frank was walking into the stadium. He turned to my cousin and commented that it sounded like a baseball bat breaking. I was aware enough to cry out to God in frustration and anger: "God, I know I am supposed to be thankful in all things, but I do not know what the BLEEP you're doing!" My quarterback, Greg, grabbed my face mask and said, "DON'T LOOK!" Then he turned green and stepped away. I was thinking, *Hey, help me up,* hoping that it was a bad sprain. Later I was told it looked like I had two knees the way my leg was distorted. It felt to me like my leg was a big water balloon with two pairs of sticks moving within it.

For 20 agonizing minutes, I laid on the field waiting for an ambulance. My father came down and asked if it hurt. I responded, "What the BLEEP do you think?" I was taken to the other team's emergency vehicle, all the while thinking, *Get me the hell out of here.* Two of my friends and favorite people of all time, Scott and Tina, came over. Tina gave me hug with tears in her eyes. "Tina," I joked, "save a dance for me at the party tonight." She smiled. Scott laughed.

On the way to the hospital in the ambulance, I felt every little crack and bump in the road as the shock was wearing off. Upon my arrival, the emergency room was short-handed so a security guard was rolling my bed around. During initial examination, nurses had already cut off my uniform and undergarments so I was naked under the thin sheets. As the security guard rolled my bed through the hall, here came Teri, the girl I had a crush on throughout high school. She was a shy girl, which I understood and liked. The security guard slowed down so I could say hi. I reached out my arm that was under my sheets not realizing that my cup was resting on the side of the bed; I bumped it and it embarrassingly landed right on her feet! The security guard rolled me toward X-ray but could not push the bed through the doors. He kept re-pushing the bed back and forth, again and again, to get it over the little speed bump, and I was grimacing in pain. The reason he could not get the bed through was because my foot fell to the right due to my twisted leg. My foot kept hitting the door jam and flexing. I grabbed the guard and said, "LOOK!" This is humorous in retrospect, but it was excruciating at the time.

My grandfather, bless his heart, came in to visit a few hours after I was settled in a room. Apparently the greatest encouragement he could think of was to pick up a couple *Playboy* magazines to cheer me up. Thanks, Grandpa. A few minutes after he left, with these magazines still on the side table, two people walked in — my pastor, Harold Fickett, and my friend Matt's dad, Dr. John MacArthur. I was horrified because these were the last two people I would have wanted to see those magazines. After that, some of my teammates showed up. Johnny G.

saw those magazines and made a beeline for them. At this point my leg was put in a half cast, like a canoe for the leg, because of the swelling, and it was incredibly sensitive to any bump or movement. Yet as Johnny bolted by, his sweater pocket caught my big toe and twisted my leg yet again. I wanted to scream in agony.

The next day after attending church, my dad came into my room and asked my friends if he could have a moment alone with me. After he closed the door and walked over to my bed, he pushed his finger into my chest and said, "I have one question: Do you remember what you said to me on the field yesterday?" From my seat there was only one safe answer — NO (although I realized I wasn't being truthful). Dad responded, "You're lucky." Then he suggested, "Now that you are on your back, there is only one direction to look, and I suggest you start doing it." UP! I felt convicted. My dad went to the door and left. At this point, my friends came back in. I realized how I felt loved by all these people whom I had chosen to turn my back on, my family included. During my time in the hospital, one of my nurses, to my surprise, remarked, "Wow, you must be really popular on campus!" I responded, "Why do you say that?" She answered, "Look how many people have come to see you." I had a full heart and realized how thankful I was to everyone who visited and showed me some love.

As much as I felt accepted and loved by my peers, I got discouraged lying there in the hospital. I was losing a massive amount of weight — maybe up to 40 pounds that week. To an athlete, that is a hard thing. The doctor explained that because of the angle of the break, there had only been a small amount of bone marrow to heal my leg at the point of the break. In fact, there would be a small chance of amputation if it did not heal properly. He set the bone well, but it did not heal properly. So six weeks later I needed surgery, during which they inserted four screws into the tibia to hold it in place while it healed. I ended up being in a cast for six months.

My senior year continued. Not being able to play basketball hurt because our coaches had expected us to win CIF. The team that did end up winning, we had beat three times the previous summer by more than 20 points each time. When my team opened the basketball season I was there for the game. I was surprised when I was announced to the crowd. The announcer said I would not be playing this year, as I stood up with my crutches. I was deeply impacted by this recognition by my school. Further, I was applauded by the coaches of the opposing team, LA Lutheran; two friends from that team (nicknamed Hicks and Spider); as well as the rest of our opponent's players. It deeply hurt not to be playing, but that was a great moment for me to be honored and respected by both my school and the rival school in basketball.

During the spring, baseball was disappointing as well. Understandably, due to my leg injury, I didn't get any playing time. Then, during a playoff game when we were playing a team whose starters all had scholarships, my coach put me in the game. I was aware that scouts from the Yankees were there; they clocked me at the hardest I'd ever thrown. I went to a full count on the first batter but walked him, trying to be cute with my pitch. After the walk, I picked that runner off of first base, then threw three fastballs and struck out the next batter. Even so, the coach decided to put in my teammate Tim for the final out. I walked off the field and gave the ball to Tim.

Remember that specific prayer before the big football game early in my senior year? I had pridefully asked God to break the leg of my teammate, then I had willfully replaced him in the game, but I was the one who broke a leg. Jesus is my Good Shepherd, and in hindsight, I trust He allowed my leg to be broken so that I would be humbled and become dependent on Him once again, just like shepherds of old used to do with their wandering sheep. The Good Shepherd brought me to His heart and carried me … until college when I wandered away again. This leads me to my next prayer.

Chapter 5

"YOU'RE THE POTTER": MY BASKETBALL STORY

From my small high school I was recruited by the football coach of a community college, College of the Canyons (COC). I decided to play basketball there instead, which was a relatively new game to me after having only played one year in high school. I had a great experience in high school with Coach Gomez and the team. Without ever playing on varsity (apart from being pulled up a couple of times for games or tournaments), I was being recruited by small schools like Westmont, Cal Lutheran, and Azusa Pacific. I thought I might have something to offer if those schools were extending me scholarships and walk-on opportunities even after coming off that broken leg experience.

I was known in high school as being a physical player, the team protector, an enforcer. Guys from other schools would come up to me before games and tournaments saying their coach had told them I would be the toughest, most physical guy they would play against that season. To be honest, I liked that reputation.

I tried to bring that persona into my new team at COC. Yet it had the effect of isolating me from others. I could not jump like I had. We had a 7 footer as well as a 6'10" guy. Where was I to even fit in? I could rebound with anyone and play defense. Coach Lee Smelser kept me around for some reason. I found a brother in Christ, Chris, who asked the whole team if there were any other Christians. I responded to Chris and his question privately because my conduct with my teammates was not a good testimony to them. Chris tried to help me. I played basketball like a linebacker. Chris explained that guys did not want to play with me in drills because they might get hurt, that I was too aggressive with them. I liked those guys on the team, but I made it hard for them to like me.

At the end of the preseason, Coach had posted the stats: Mine were 80% (8/10) from the free-throw line and 92% (11/12) from the field. These were great numbers for me, but that was only for four to six preseason games. Coach came to me and said, "You pass the ball and play defense really well. We are playing Pierce College next week. Your buddy from high school, Scott Ardavanis, plays point there. I want you to play point guard against him." I was shocked. Scott was an amazing dribbler and shooter, and I did not know how to dribble at that level. I had played center in high school. That week, I contacted Scott and asked for his help; he taught me to dribble in his backyard. Then I went home and cleaned out my family's garage, turned out the lights, and practiced dribbling. I kept to myself the fact that I would go head up with him. I had decided that there was no way I was going to play over-the-top physical, like I usually did, against Scott, but at the end of the first half he threw an elbow at me and then it was "on like Donkey Kong." I loved Scott; he would become one of three guys I would say is a spiritual hero to me. He was a true basketball player, and I was not. That game, we battled it out on the court. Off the court, all these years later, he is still one of my closest friends.

After that game, Coach Smelser called me into his office; he wanted me to red-shirt. At the time I didn't even know what that meant. He explained that it meant I would not be on the team for games; I still did not know if I was to attend practices or work out. This was right before Christmas break so I decided to enjoy the break because I didn't think I needed to be at practices.

Personally and spiritually during that time, I was like a lost sheep, wandering again and wearing a mask to cover over my true identity as a follower of Christ. Thankfully God was working in my heart. I was close to my youth pastor and went to his house on New Year's Eve. Just before midnight, I was lying on his floor completely prostrate, praying, "Father, You are the Potter, and I am the clay." I pictured myself on the Potter's wheel — what a wobbly mess I had become. I begged God for forgiveness once again and asked the Potter to remold me into what He wanted; essentially I was recommitting my life to Him in that moment.

In my mind's eye, I pictured His hand coming through the middle of me as the vessel, like a karate chop, cracking the clay in half. Then I saw His fist coming down on top and smashing everything down. Finally, I pictured His hands kneading me like someone making bread, squashing the air out of the clay to keep it fresh and moldable so He could remold me into something useful. That New Year's Eve was a night of refreshing prayer that I will never forget.

January 1 was full of football games on television with friends at my friend's house. My friends were drinking beers while I was grasping for my friend's father's porn magazines under the coffee table. We eventually got bored and went to the park near his house for some pick-up football. We were having fun when, all of a sudden, Jim was in the grasp of John, our fullback in high school. Jim was being spun around and around like a helicopter prop. As I bolted toward him, I suddenly remembered that I was not in my football gear so I turned my head away. This left my back facing him just as his knee struck the lumbar area of my spine. I was in pain but, trying to be tough, got up for the next play. They hiked the ball, but I could not move. Terrible pain was flooding my body in that moment. It felt like a water balloon had burst in my back and someone was pouring a whistling teapot of boiling water down the back of both of my legs. John and the guys got me back to his house where I sat patiently in the most comfortable position I could find. About 45 minutes later, John took me to the emergency room.

Because the pain was so bad, I told the ER doctor that if he could get rid of this pain, he could break both of my legs. He looked at me in confusion, like, "Do you know what you are saying?" and I said, "Yes, sir, I know what a broken leg feels like." The X-rays revealed fractures in my 3rd and 5th lumbar vertebrae. Afterward, my mom told me repeatedly that she was praying for healing. Miraculously, a week later another set of X-rays revealed no fractures. The doctor was dumbfounded; he tried to come up with some excuses, which fell on deaf ears. We knew it was a miracle. Three weeks later I was skiing in Mammoth. Although I had promised my parents I would not, my rebellion continued, and they knew I took my skis with me. In hindsight, I realized that experience was the hand I had visualized during my New Year's Eve prayer, coming and cracking the middle of my body (the clay vessel).

Six weeks later, God's fist of discipline came down. I was back at John's house. We decided to go somewhere but take two cars. John was driving his, a cool cherry-red Camaro, and I was in my red Honda Prelude, which I was too tall for, and had the sunroof open. After stopping at the stop sign in front of his house, John took off quickly to get out of the way of the car he saw coming. I was just getting in my car, getting it started, when John went to the left. Because I was trying to catch up with him, I did not take the time to stop. I hit the gas and went right through the stop sign. As I went around the corner (a blind intersection), John had just cleared the intersection. Because of what he saw coming, he was looking in the rearview mirror saying to himself, "Don't go, Buck" — but I had. A young priest was driving a new BMW at almost twice the speed limit. His BMW, going almost 60 mph, hit my driver's door, lifting my Honda up. John said he watched me being lifted from my seat and saw my head sticking out of the sunroof, fearing that he was going to witness his friend being decapitated in front of him. In his words, it was like an angel pushed me back down into the car so quickly. My car slid almost 100 feet, hitting the curb across the street from his house.

On impact my reaction had been to reach for my unbuckled seat belt, or likely I had already reached for it when I saw the car coming toward me. When I woke from getting knocked out, John was checking on me, telling me not to move. Firemen and paramedics were there immediately. For sure I had my bell rung. A paramedic asked me my name; my response was, "Can you come back to that in a minute? I know I know it." Immediately he called for the firemen saying, "Come here, you gotta see this!" Then he shouted, "I've never seen this before." That made me nervous so I began checking all my limbs. He reached in with a knife and cut the seat belt that had brought me back into the car. On impact, I had grabbed the seat belt and threw it down and it clicked into the passenger's seat belt receptor. The amazing thing is that it precisely hit the target and saved my life. I believe in angels and miracles, and here was another miracle in my life — a seat belt snapping into the connector that it's not supposed to and fit in backwards.

I still had a huge bump on the left side of my head from the sunroof. My elbow was cut from the glass in the driver's door. And my knee was punctured from the side mirror adjuster. Decades later I would drive by Louise Street and could still see the marks on the curb from my totaled car. Snap (in half), Crackle (in the car), and now for the Pop!

After the accident, I kept revisiting the prayer I made on New Year's Eve. Another six weeks went by, and I was back at work at Six Flags Magic Mountain where I was a Senior Lead, second in charge of our food area just past the Log Jammer and across from the concert venue. The other Senior Lead was a high school buddy, Loren. We worked well together. Kim, our boss, was getting ready to depart, and it would likely soon be Loren or me in charge of this food area. The two of us agreed that we would be fine with either one of us getting the position.

Unfortunately, when Kim left, a young lady from another part of the park was brought in to be in charge. Loren and I were disappointed, but we loved our jobs. But within a day she demoted both Loren and me. I was angry, and so was Loren! Other people were upset, too.

What happened next were a series of incidents that spun out of control. At first this young lady brought in her friends to fill our spots, trying to establish herself in her new area. Then she started getting threats via notes and phone calls. I honestly felt bad for her, but I did think she brought it on herself and I was still upset. Loren and I would talk with some empathy, but neither one of us had a clue who was making these threats. Next her purse got stolen and was left in pieces on her desk. Then the tires to her car were knifed in the staff parking lot. We knew this was wrong; both of us questioned each other, but neither of us were involved.

Because these actions were obviously wrong, I went to my grandfather Chuck, who had worked in security at the park for a long time, to find out if he knew what was going on. He shared with me the Sheriff's Department was on it now. I told him to let them know that I would help in any way that I could. "OK," he said with a smile.

The escalating situation culminated when the young woman's car was somewhere in the Santa Clarita Valley where Six Flags is located, and someone attached a bomb to the bottom of it. The bomb squad came and cleared three city blocks. The bomb ended up being a fake, but this poor young woman, what she must have been going through. I honestly felt really bad for her.

The next week I received a summons from the Sheriff's Department. When I saw it in the mailbox, I thought maybe

Grandpa Chuck told them I wanted to help. When I arrived at the Sheriff's station, I was calm and excited to help. After checking in at the counter, I was quickly escorted down a hallway by a lady officer. I was thinking, *Good, a lady cop, I am comfortable talking with ladies.* About halfway down the hall, I noticed my shadow was engulfed by one bigger than my own, and I am 6'5" and not a small person.

The two sheriff's deputies sat me down and began by saying, "The only way you are leaving here today is …" In that split second I was thinking, *What?! I came to help you guys!* The male sheriff said they knew it was me and that I should just confess. "You're wrong, sir," I said with a frustrated tone. The lady was playing the good cop; the big guy put his billy club down on the desk and turned as if he were walking out the door. I almost made the biggest mistake of my life when I nearly reached for his billy club to hand it to him. Thank God I did not touch it.

During this time I was thinking, *Oh brother, my mom is going to be pissed at me.* Next I was forced to take a handwriting test; my hand was shaking as I took the test. These two sheriff's deputies said that as far as they could tell, my handwriting matched the notes that the young woman had received, even though at the time, the handwriting specialist was not present. After about 10 minutes, which felt like an hour, they said, "The only way you are going home today is for you to give us your fingerprints." At this point I was getting frustrated, asking, "What if I don't?" They replied, "Then we are booking you for attempted murder right now." I figured I should cooperate and gave them my fingerprints. Ultimately, I was free and cleared because the fingerprints did not match. Even so, this incident definitely squeezed the air out of me.

The author of the Book of Hebrews writes about God's discipline, sharing that He disciplines those He loves as His sons. Hebrews 12:11 (NIV) says, *"No discipline seems pleasant at the time, but painful. Later on, however, it produces a harvest of righteousness and peace for those who have been trained by it."* In my life during this year, although I didn't fully embrace it, God was working His discipline to bring me to humble dependence on Him.

Chapter 6

"HURT ME AGAIN": MY BASEBALL STORY

I was back at COC, working two jobs and trying to make the COC baseball team. The head coach was Mike Gillespie, one of the best coaches ever in college baseball. Rainy days were fun because Coach did lectures for more than two hours teaching about the game. I loved it!

After breaking my leg and fracturing my back, I had lost my fastball. During this time frame, for three summers, I played for another team called the Grace Saints. I was their starting pitcher for the latter two years, and I finally learned how to pitch, not just throwing hard like I had done my whole life.

Coach Mike at COC wanted me to throw side arm. I wish I would have trusted him then, but because I am 6'5", I was convinced I should just be throwing downhill. I was enjoying the whole experience. One Saturday I was scheduled to work, and because I had pitched the game before, I knew I would not be pitching that day. I told the COC captains to let Coach know I had to work and wouldn't be at the game. That Sunday I pitched for the Saints and threw a one hitter through six innings. The Valley College coach was in the stands; one of his pitchers brought him to the game. My teammate Darrel told me the Valley College coach had watched me and was interested in me playing for him.

The next day, Monday, I was at Coach Mike's bulletin board at COC to see the cut list. I was surprised to see my name there — printed bigger than all the other names. My thoughts were, *I am gone! I need to find somewhere to play.* I decided against going to Valley College and immediately started baseball at Pierce College with a group of friends; Scott, Matt, and Rod were all guys committed to growing in their faith as well. However, I was still taking classes at COC. One day shortly thereafter, Coach Mike saw me on campus and told me he had been hoping I would come by his office, that his intent by putting me on the cut list was just to get into my head, not really to cut me. (I never knew if the captains gave him the message that I wouldn't be at that game.) I told Coach Mike about my Sunday outing playing for the Saints with the Valley College coach in the stands, and said I was going to Valley College (a white lie).

At Pierce we had some good ministry going on with Scott, Matt, Rod, and myself. The coaches there, Coach Lyons and Coach Murray, called me into the dugout, asking, "Why are the guys wanting to talk with you during hitting and shagging?" I responded, "Coach, I am just telling them about my relationship with God, that's all." "Nothing illegal?" one coach asked. "No, sir, just about God," I responded. Even so, they did not want any more groups around me as we shagged balls.

My junior high coach, Mr. York, became our pitching coach at Pierce. I was surprised he had remembered me. Both my leg and my back had healed strongly, and I was sent with my new team to Antelope Valley College to start a game on the mound. I remember Matt driving Rod and me out to that ballfield, and while we were driving, I found a metal ball that weighed a pound or two in his car and did some shoulder exercises with it. When we arrived, it was cold and windy, but all of a sudden, amazing myself, my fastball was back, on location and popping the catcher's glove. After the game, Matt got in the car and said to me, "I have not seen you dominate a game like that since our high school days." At that point I had been #12 on the depth chart but now all of a sudden moved to #2 after that game.

The next Monday Coach Lyons and Coach Murray shouted to me and said, "Come here!" "Yes, sir," I responded. They proceeded to say, "We were not at the game two days ago, but since then we have had 14 scouts call and inquire about you. They will be coming today, and they all want to see you throw. Are you good for an inning?" I was stunned and said, "YES! Who is coming again?" All 14 scouts.

A few innings into the game, I had made my way to the bullpen. I saw Matt and Rod in the middle infield; I was always comfortable with those two behind me. I took a deep breath, started throwing to the catcher, and paused to say a prayer. I prayed, "God, if it is not Your plan for me to play professional baseball and use it as a platform to serve You, hurt me, get me out of here, and I will go serve You as a youth minister. YOUR WILL BE DONE." I wound up to throw to my catcher, heard the crack of the bat, looked up and saw a blistering line drive into the bullpen. It hit a tree, ricocheted off, and hit me in the head, moving my hat from its position. I looked up and said, "Close, God, but not close enough." I then turned to catch the ball from my catcher. He had already thrown it, and just as I turned my head, the ball hit me square in the nose. All of this happened within a second after I had finished my prayer.

My nose was bleeding profusely, and blood covered my shirt. I walked by my coaches. "What happened?" one asked. "I know you will not understand, but God does not want me here," I said as I walked to my truck. I threw my glove and spikes into the bed of the truck as I checked my nose to see if it was broken. I got a tap on my shoulder from a scout, "Mike, did you just quit?" "Yes, George, I did," I replied. "OK, the San Francisco Giants would like to sign you then. I have been watching you for three years as I coached against the Saints. Changing speeds you were great; now your fastball — where did that come from?" I simply said, "It's back." George, who happened to be the number-one signing scout in San Francisco Giants history, put a folder on the truck with contracts in it. I said, "Yesterday, I would have pricked my finger and signed it in blood, but today I cannot." "But," I asked, "how much would I have gotten?" George answered, "Just a standard contract for minor league ball, no signing bonus."

God showed Himself very clearly to me in His answer to my whispered prayer for direction that day. His grace and mercy have always been faithful.

PART THREE:
LESSONS I
LEARNED
THE HARD WAY

Chapter 7

TWO CHOICES IN RESPONSE TO TRIALS AND INJURIES

In my life, God has shown Himself to me through prayer. I believe one of God's purposes for prayer is to build our faith. Because of these three athletic experiences and other answered prayers, how could I ever doubt His presence in my life?

God's goal is exaltation, but the question that must be asked is, exaltation of whom? Think about the Old Testament stories (Noah, Moses, David, Jonah, etc.). Who is the Hero in those stories? God is! Who would you have Him exalt? You? Me? God's ultimate goal is always to exalt Himself.

Both followers of Christ and those who do not follow Christ have shared with me that when inflicted by an injury, they realize that God is trying to get their attention. C.S. Lewis said, *"Pain insists upon being attended to. God whispers to us in our pleasures, speaks in our consciences, but shouts in our pains. It is his megaphone to rouse a deaf world."* Like many, I became unresponsive to God's whispers in my life. As I continued to wander and ignore God's whispers through my parents, friends, and the Bible, God shouted through injuries to get my attention.

So then, how do we deal with moments of pain, destroyed dreams, and heartache? There are always two paths to choose from to deal with your injury: your way or God's way.

Bottom line, God loves you. As Hebrews 12:6–7 says, *"For those whom the Lord loves He disciplines, and He scourges every son whom He receives. It is for discipline that you endure; God deals with you as with sons; for what son is there whom his father does not discipline?"* God's discipline is not purposeless. True discipline serves to rehabilitate and refine, not to punish.

Human Beings' Typical Response to Pain

Let's first talk about the path that is **NOT** God's way to deal with your circumstances of pain, the typical way of response. Here's what I did (what I think most people do). First, I cursed God; I blamed Him for the circumstance I was in. Second, I nursed it; I blew it up and magnified it. Last, I rehearsed it; I went over and over it in my mind, dwelling on it so that it consumed me. Have you or are you now taking the steps down this path that I took, the steps of curse, nurse, and rehearse?

Let's consider these three steps, the typical way of response:

CURSE – Are you blaming God for your pain? Cursing Him? This is usually the immediate response when an injury happens, for both believers and non-believers. I have heard it from my own lips and those of many others in that moment of pain.

I remember being in my truck driving from my parents' house to San Diego State University. I cussed and cursed at God for two-and-a-half hours because my aspirations of being a professional athlete had been destroyed. I yelled at Him,

"Do You know what You are doing? You're a dream-giver and a dream-stealer!" My language would have made a sailor blush. Funny that I rolled my windows down, thinking it would be easier for God to hear me.

At the end of that drive, I pulled over and watched one of the most beautiful sunsets I had ever seen. God ministered to me through that sunset. I realized that beautiful sunsets do not come without clouds, some very dark. In that moment something switched. I wrote a poem reflecting the warmth of the hues, reaching out as far as I could see and embracing me with the Father's love. This was the day I started trusting God with my pain.

After penning this poem, in hindsight it hit me most of all, who wants me to curse God? Satan does. I do not want to be siding with the enemy and getting trapped in his subtle schemes meant for my destruction. God's goodness drew me back to Him through that painted sky, and I asked for forgiveness yet another time from my Father in heaven.

NURSE – Are you turning the pain into something so much bigger than it probably is? Are you perhaps worshiping your pain? We tend to magnify it — the proverbial "making a mountain out of a molehill." It begins to consume us when we nurse it.

REHEARSE – Are you playing the pain over and over and over again in your mind? Does it dominate your thinking and affect other areas of your life? It is like we are pitching a tent and living alone with this memory of disappointment. This could easily, and often unknowingly, turn into something God's Word warns us of: planting a root of bitterness. Hebrews

12:15 warns us to make sure *that no root of bitterness springing up causes trouble, and by it many be defiled.*" I am not sure I was totally aware of this, nor would I ever have admitted it, but after a decade or so, looking in the rearview mirror, I realized I had let a root of bitterness entangle around my heart. Others who knew me well in college could tell you this was true; my insecurities were at high tide in my life.

In some cases, people want to stay angry, thinking this will bring protection against further disappointment; however, it turns out this is a facade. This reminds me of an example that comes from the Polynesian culture. On the walls and sometimes the ceilings of their huts, warriors would hang visual reminders, focal points, of pain in their lives to wake up to every day, so as to stay angry. Mentally, I did that. Are you living with memories of the pain hanging on the walls of your mind? Do you fuel your anger, ignorant of its danger? (Notice that anger is one letter away from danger.)

Because of my insecurities that surfaced from my shattered dreams, I tried to prove to everyone that I was the real deal. I tried to tell anyone who would listen how good I could have been, whom I played with, and so on. I sought to exalt myself for consolation. It took quite a few years for me to realize that it's God's love that makes you the real deal. He values you so much that His Son shed His blood for you. That alone is the greatest trade ever: Jesus' blood for your sins.

According to James 1:2–4, *"Consider it all joy, my brethren, when you encounter various trials, knowing that the testing of your faith produces endurance. And let endurance have its perfect result, so that you may be perfect and complete, lacking in nothing."* We are guaranteed to be tested, and our reaction to those situations will reveal where our faith really stands.

This passage by the apostle James paints the picture of the Refiner's fire that purges the impurities out of our lives to make us more like the Refiner, Jesus Christ. The original meaning in the Greek for "testing" refers to a process where a refiner turns up the heat by adding logs to the fire under a pot of precious metal that is being purified. It is allowed to cool and the dross (impurities) is scraped off; then the heat is turned up again by adding another log to the fire. This process continues until the refiner can see his clear reflection, like a mirror, in the purified metal. Christ is committed to purifying us so that we reflect His image. Unfortunately, it is usually painful when the heat is turned up. But the reward is worth enduring the process.

C.T. Studd, one of the greatest cricket players in the late 1880s, turned missionary and one of my spiritual heroes, wrote a short book called *The Chocolate Soldier* (you can listen to it read on YouTube). The analogy in the book that spoke to me is that when the heat in life is turned up as we are being refined, we are not to be chocolate soldiers and melt in the moment, but strong men and women of faith. The apostle Paul tells us, *"Be on the alert, stand firm in the faith, act like men, be strong"* (1 Corinthians 16:13).

A Different Response

There's another path to travel down, God's way.

REVERSE – We need to reverse course instead of just allowing the natural human response, which is to curse it, nurse it, and rehearse it. God's Word has a lot to say about dealing with difficult circumstances. A passage that has been so profound in my life that I can recite it in my sleep is Philippians 4:4–9. The Lord has branded it on my heart.

> *Rejoice in the Lord always; again I will say, rejoice! Let your gentle spirit be known to all men. The Lord is near. Be anxious for nothing, but in everything by prayer and supplication with thanksgiving let your requests be made known to God. And the peace of God, which surpasses all comprehension, will guard your hearts and your minds in Christ Jesus. Finally, brethren, whatever is true, whatever is honorable, whatever is right, whatever is pure, whatever is lovely, whatever is of good repute, if there is any excellence and if anything worthy of praise, dwell on these things. The things you have learned and received and heard and seen in me, practice these things, and the God of peace will be with you.*

Let's explore this passage together verse by verse in order to unpack this different response to pain, God's way.

Philippians 4:4
"Rejoice in the Lord always; again I will say, rejoice."

The apostle Paul wrote these words from prison. When I first heard this, I remember thinking, *This is crazy, ludicrous! Put down your pom-poms, please. The last thing I need is that cheerleader's voice saying, "Rejoice, Rejoice."* Another quick reaction at first glance.

I've heard it said that "rejoice" means to bathe yourself in joy. To let joy surround you. Then it hit me: Three small words in this verse are the key — ***"in the Lord."*** It's not rejoicing in the injury. Rather, I am to find my joy in the Lord by trusting Him, trusting in what He has ordained to happen to me. This is the same for you, in your situation. It helps to put your eyes back on the Lord instead of the situation.

Being the young man I was, I would often go hide in a hot shower; I called it my "shower of power." I would let the water pour over me and think of God's truths from His Word. I would bathe in those truths — that I am His child, redeemed, justified, reconciled to Him because of His love, that I have the fruit of the Spirit — and pray that I would truly find my identity in Him instead of whichever sport I was playing at the time. To be honest, the shower was also a safe place to let tears flow that I didn't want anyone else to see.

Tears can be a healing thing. For me, sadly, at age 11, I had a Little League coach, whom I respected, approach me and tell me I could be the best player in the league if I would just stop crying and complaining about every call. As an incorrect response, for over a decade I did not shed a tear. My wife can tell you about the time outside her dorm room when all that pent-up emotion burst, and in an hour I made up for what I had been holding in for years.

The key points we can take away from Philippians 4:4 are the following:

1. Focus on the Lord, not your circumstance. Remember Hebrews 12:2, "fixing our eyes on Jesus."

2. Take a "shower" under the shower head of God's love; imagine all His love pouring out over you.

3. Rejoice in who you are in Christ through His Word.

4. Find your identity in Him alone. (Read more on this in Chapter 10, "A Trophy of Grace.")

Philippians 4:5a
"Let your gentle [forbearing] spirit be known to all men"

Another word that is translated in the Scriptures for "forbearing" is "gentleness," a fruit of the Holy Spirit from Galatians 5:22–23. This can be more accurately understood as part of the fruit of the Holy Spirit (not nine different fruits), one of the nine flavors He is committed to creating in us.

But I do like the word "forbearing." Here in Philippians 4:5 it means to "put up with," and there is a lot we need to put up with in relationship with others, for example, people's clichés said in response to our situations, knowing they would not have said what they did if they had experienced anything similar. These words can come in the form of unsolicited advice, teasing, devaluing comments, and other very hurtful things. The phrase "Sticks and stones may break my bones, but names will never hurt me" is one of the biggest lies ever. When it comes to hurtful words, most of us can remember who said what, where, and when.

Scripture paints pictures of "gentleness" such as a mother with her child, a lamb going to slaughter (Jesus Christ), and in Proverbs, "gentle words" being those that wield great power. This forbearing/gentle spirit is what we are commanded to let be seen in us and through us even in the midst of our trial.

Philippians 4:5b
"The Lord is near"

Philippians 4:5b reminds us of the amazing truth that God is near to us and never leaves us. In other words, He has our back. When we show a forbearing and gentle spirit, He shows up and exalts Himself.

I once heard a story from the pulpit that illustrates this point perfectly:

A world-champion boxer, a bare knuckle champion who had retired, found himself working in the coal mines. Unfortunately it was a time of segregation in our country. This boxer was a black man, and a white man commented to his lunch buddies, "Isn't he a Christian? And aren't Christians supposed to turn the other cheek when struck on one?" Getting up from his table, he walked up to this ex-professional fighter, clenched his fist, and struck the ex-champion of the world in the jaw. I, personally, think there was something other than coffee in this man's thermos.

Now what would we expect from a trained fighter who would have been taught not to think but to react, and react swiftly? Most of us would expect him to react with his favorite combo! And really, he had the right to, after being struck without cause. I have been blessed to be in a few dojos in my life, and although martial arts are called self-defense, the best fighters in the dojos are not thinking defense, they are not waiting to react. These fighters are trained in tactical offensive explosions.

So how did our ex-boxer champion respond? Jab, cross, uppercut, hook … and many would say rightfully so? No, he responded not with his world-class fighting skills but with these words, *"I forgive you as the Father has forgiven me."* What? Wow! The hurtful man did not get what he deserved but what he needed.

Over the next few days, the man could not get that phrase out of his head. Without an apology he approached the ex-champion three days later and asked, "What did you mean, that you forgive me as the Father has forgiven you?" The boxer explained the gospel message to this man who had struck him on the cheek and, ultimately, saw this man come to Christ. The Lord was near.

Have you ever been in a situation where you have humbly yielded your right and then seen God show up and do something unexpected and pull on the heartstrings of another's heart? I have witnessed it and have experienced this truth as well in my life.

Question for you: Imagine yourself as a glass. When you are bumped in life, what spills out of you? What is it that comes out first?

Philippians 4:6a
"Be anxious for nothing"

This is a command. Stress and anxiety go hand in hand. Stress often exhibits itself physically, for example, tight muscles, aching teeth or jaw, upset stomach, and so on. Anxiety is the mental form of stress, the brooding fear of a future contingency or possible happenings in your life. Anxiety is also the opposite of peace; peace is yet another flavor of the fruit of the Holy Spirit. Anxiety, to be honest, is sin. It means we are not trusting God with the situation He is taking us through. We are caught up in worry (Matthew 6:25–34).

Philippians 4:6b
"but in everything by prayer and supplication with thanksgiving let your requests be made known to God."

The apostle Paul, being Holy Spirit–led, was a great writer and speaker. In Philippians 4:6b, he says the same thing basically four times. Four different ways he says to take your anxiety to God.

PRAYER – Human beings are the only creature God created to have a relationship with Him. At different times over the years, I have been asked, "How do you pray?" While many might reply, "Duh," it is actually a serious and good question. My response is illustrated by my role as a father. I want my children to talk to me respectfully, but I also want them to know that they can come to me, crawl up into my lap, and pour out their hearts. Just like that, I tell people to come to God and just be honest when they talk to Him. And, as we are instructed, we should pray in the name of Jesus Christ.

SUPPLICATION – This is a picture of humbling oneself before a king, as a knight would have bowed to his king. In this case, it's the King of kings.

THANKSGIVING – Paul tells us to have a heart of gratitude and an attitude of gratitude knowing that God hears you and is in complete control. Many times God allows things to happen that you and I will never understand on this side of heaven; trust Him! Be reminded that Jesus Himself is praying for you in heaven. The Holy Spirit is taking your prayers to the throne room of God. When we have thanksgiving in our hearts, it exemplifies trust.

Let me share one of the greatest tools that I have used and also found helpful with other people when going through difficult circumstances. I ask them to take some time to ask God what they have to be thankful for and then to write down what comes to mind. Pray for God to show you what to be thankful for. I realize this may sound ridiculous, but God shows up in those moments and reveals what we can be thankful for. I have gained a fresh perspective when I have done this. I would encourage you to do this as well.

LET YOUR REQUESTS BE MADE KNOWN – This is awesome! God is saying, "Come share what you want, share your thoughts with Me." Be honest with Him about your burdens, needs, and desires.

Philippians 4:7a
"And the peace of God"

Here we are reminded that God is the only true Source of peace; nowhere else can it be found. Try as much as you would like, but let me save you some time. Ultimately, He is the only source of true peace. The following story is one of my favorite illustrations of peace.

There once was a king who offered a prize to the artist who could paint the best picture of peace. Many artists tried and submitted their work. The king looked at all of the pictures. There were only two he really liked, and he had to choose between them.

One picture was of a calm lake, perfectly mirroring the peaceful, towering mountains all around it. Overhead was blue sky with fluffy, white clouds. This painting was the favorite of all who saw it. *Truly*, they thought, *this was the perfect picture of peace.*

The other paintings had mountains, too, but these were rugged and bare. Above was an angry sky from which rain fell and in which lightning struck. Down the side of one mountain tumbled a foaming waterfall. A less peaceful picture would be difficult to imagine, it seemed. But when the king looked closely, he saw beside the waterfall a tiny bush growing from a crack in the rock. In the bush a mother bird had built her nest. There, in the midst of the rush of a violent storm and of angry water, sat the mother bird on her nest in perfect peace.

Which picture would you have selected? The king chose the second picture. Do you know why?

The king explained, "Peace does not mean to be in a place where there is no noise, trouble, or hard work. Peace means to be in the midst of all these things and still be calm in your heart. This is the real meaning of peace."

As the saying goes, "You can know peace if you know God, but no God, no peace." Why? Because God is the only true Source of peace.

Philippians 4:7b
"which surpasses all comprehension, will guard your hearts and your minds in Christ Jesus."

I have my own personal moment with experiencing the peace that surpasses all comprehension and that guarded my heart and my mind; as is often the case, it came through one of my most difficult circumstances so far in life.

It was the very beginning of May, 1998. We lived in Hawaii at the time. Five nights earlier, my wife, Alison, had bumped me in the middle of the night and said, "My water broke." I responded, "Not funny, let me sleep." She was at the end of her 28th week of pregnancy with our second baby. We rushed to the hospital and admitted Alison. The doctors gave her medicine to prevent contractions (that worked only for four days) and a shot to help the development of the baby's lungs. I was in a place of the greatest anxiety I'd ever experienced.

Friends of ours, Dave and Mary Shoji, cared for our 3-year-old, Chris, and Alison's mom flew out from Los Angeles. On the night of May 3, our doctor Gary Fujimoto, whom we loved and trusted, a brother in Christ, came in. Dr. Fujimoto said he had been praying for wisdom from God (as we are told in James 1:5) regarding the need to take the baby out at this time. Alison had started running a fever that day at the hospital, so they took her off the medicine that was preventing contractions. When Dr. Fujimoto came in, he shared how he had been praying, and at that very moment Alison had a contraction, causing the baby's heart to go into distress, plus the ongoing issue of the fever. So the decision was made for Alison to have her second C-section. This was another anxious circumstance because they needed to do a vertical cut on the uterus to get the baby out more quickly. Very early in the morning on May 4, Emily Kanani (named after both grandmothers) was born. She was a "booming" 3 pounds, 1 ounce and 15 inches, which seemed so small to us.

With my best friend and wife (one in the same) in the hospital's ICU and downstairs my baby daughter in the NICU, I was filled with anxiety. I moved into highly protective mode. Every muscle in my body was tense, laser-like looks were flowing through my eyes, and I had no tolerance of anything ("Do not look at me funny," "Do not bump me," etc.). I was a piece of dynamite, lit and ready to blow up at anything. I was chiefly concerned about Alison, but as a mom, she was concerned about Emily and Chris. I was not sure if I even wanted to get attached to Emily, even though in truth I already was. This was a useless attempt to protect my heart from the worst situation I could imagine ... our baby girl not surviving. Emily was a fighter from the start; she pulled out the ventilation tube that first night and breathed on her own. The nurses kept saying things like, "You got a tough little girl," "You got a fighter," and "Watch out for this one!" (Years later we realized they were right!)

I picked up Chris from the Shojis' house and went back to the hospital. At only 3 years old, my little son sensed something was bothering me deeply; the anxiety was obviously spilling out of me. Before we got to the NICU, Chris stepped in front of his 6'5" dad and said, with his big blue eyes peering up at me and in a gentle voice, "Stop, Dad. You need to pray." Chris was right! I stopped and prayed with my son and asked God to take control of my anxiety, stress, and sin. Miraculously, for the next four weeks I was in that bubble of peace that surpasses all comprehension. There is no way I could explain it to anyone; it was truly what no words can describe. IT WAS UNBELIEVABLE!

Because she was recovering from the C-section, which included a broken rib from the baby being taken out so quickly, and they had rushed Emily to the NICU, Alison didn't even get to see her baby girl until the day after she was born. Alison was finally allowed to hold Emily for the first time exactly a week later on Mother's Day.

We had an amazing experience. It was hard, but God showed up completely for us and built our faith. During our hospital stay, we were even able to minister to a lady who had just had her fourth premature baby; her little girl was only 1 pound, 14 ounces. Tragically, her husband could not handle the stress again, and as a result, he left her alone in the hospital with little Hailey (and I mean "left her" in the sense of never to return). In a beautiful act of God's grace, our families celebrated both girls' birthdays together a year later. Peace is so real! Know God, know His peace; no God, no peace.

So I challenge you: Will you pause from reading this right now and take time to bring all of your life to God and trust Him with your situations of anxiety and fear? God wants to protect the very thing we say people lose at times like these — their hearts and their minds. Let Him guard you with true peace from the only true Source: God.

To finish our passage, let's look at the apostle Paul's wonderful challenges in Philippians 4:8–9. Remember when I said earlier how when we rehearse things so much, it dominates our thinking and can even affect how our body functions? Let's look at what God's Word describes what to dwell on.

<u>Philippians 4:8–9</u>
"Finally, brethren, whatever is true, whatever is honorable, whatever is right, whatever is pure, whatever is lovely, whatever is of good repute, if there is any excellence and if anything worthy of praise, dwell on these things. The things you have learned and received and heard and seen in me, practice these things, and the God of peace will be with you."

Paul, who went through trials beyond anything most of us have ever experienced (see 2 Corinthians 11:23–33), tells us to practice dwelling on the right things. This means rehearsing those things in our mind. Just like an athlete, even at the highest level, needs to physically practice the fundamentals, we need to continually fill our minds and hearts with these truths.

God often chooses pain to get our attention. In those trials and pain, humans typically respond in two ways. There is definitely a choice. We can choose to curse and blame God, nurse our anger and let it consume us, and rehearse the bitterness. But there is a better and different response. Philippians 4:4–9 outlines the steps in the better choice, God's way, which is to humbly turn to God in our circumstances, through prayer and thanksgiving, dwelling on what is good. In this path there is peace.

PART FOUR:
CRITICAL TRUTHS UNDERSTOOD

Chapter 8
THE DOOR TO HEAVEN
For those who want to know Jesus Christ

Jesus' work and purpose in life was to redeem the lost. Because of Adam's sin, all have been separated from God (Romans 5:19). Jesus is referred to as the "door" in John 10 four times. Therefore, it is presumed that there is a wall for there to be a need for a door. We only find a door where there is a wall. This wall separates man from God because of His wrath toward us, a holy side and a side for those not holy (all of mankind) thanks to Adam.

This wall is unscalable, although many will try; for example, the mentality of some is that they will try to work their way to heaven. Man was created to have fellowship with the Almighty God, who is unapproachable apart from a relationship with His Son Jesus Christ and the work of the Holy Spirit. People have tried on their own, but no one can win the love of God apart from entering through Jesus Christ, the Door.

There are four things I have learned about the Door from a book by Roy and Revel Hession called *We Would See Jesus.*[1] This title states the purpose of life for all of us, in my opinion.) Let's explore these four aspects of the Door, that is, Jesus, our way to fellowship with the Living God:

---

1. Roy and Revel Hession, *We Would See Jesus* (Fort Washington, PA: Christian Literature Crusade, 1958).

1. The Door Is Always Open

If the door is not open, it is not Jesus! There are those who make you feel like you need to perform to a certain standard or else you will never arrive. Jesus Christ is always open to you whenever and wherever you are in life. You cannot get any better for Jesus. You are broken, that is, separated, until you enter through Him as the Door.

I hear over and over again, "I need to get things right first before I come to Him." In truth, just come as you are and He will help you get things right; in fact, He will make you righteous and justify you and reconcile you to Himself. You cannot "get right" apart from Him. Through the shedding of His blood on the cross, when you trust Him with your life, He makes you right before the Almighty Father. Even our ability to trust Him to walk through the Door is the work of the Holy Spirit.

He loves you; that is why He has made a door for you. When Jesus was up on the cross, He said, "It is finished …" and bowed His head. When He died, the veil in the temple was torn from top to bottom, opening up the tabernacle (tent) for all mankind to enter. This was a symbol that man could be back in good standing with God by the grace that He offers you and me. It was a veil (a wall) that separated man from the Holy of Holies, where the presence of God was within the tent. God opened the door for mankind. This door into His presence has been made by Jesus Christ alone, and it is open to anyone! In Jesus' own words, *"I am the way, and the truth, and the life; no one comes to the Father but through Me"* (John 14:6).

2. The Door Is Street Level

Jesus put the door where anyone can reach it and enter. You and I have a tendency to put the door someplace where it is out of reach. We make it unattainable, unreachable, but that is not Jesus. This door is for anyone on the streets of life who needs a Savior, anyone who needs to be rescued and can acknowledge that they have a need for a Savior. The door is right there, one step away.

3. The Door Is Low

Jesus' door is for those willing to come through humbly; we are made to bow down. You and I will only come through when we humbly recognize our need of a Lord and Savior. As Jesus bowed His head before He died, we too must bow our heads in humility and repentance to Him and acknowledge our need for Him. We must submit ourselves to our new Lord, giving up our right to be the lord of our own lives.

4. The Door Is Narrow

Jesus has made this door narrow so that only one can come through at a time. What I mean is, there are no grandchildren in heaven (that is, you don't get in because your parents are Christian). This is an individual decision; no one can make it for you. It is your choice to make Jesus the Lord, Master, and King of your life and let Him save you from the wrath of God the Father that is due to each one of us.

He is a just God; we deserve to be on the other side of the wall where we started. Yet He is also a loving God; that is why

He has made a door for us to come through.

Saying a prayer does not save you, but it is an expression to God of your faith in Him. God is not looking at our words when we pray; rather, He always looks at and knows the true status of our hearts.

A prayer of confession of faith may look something like this:

> *Dear Jesus, I am desperate for You. I admit I have lived my life independent of You from the day I was born, and I acknowledge that self-centeredness as sin. I thank You, Father, for Your Son and His shedding of blood that I might have a relationship with You. I ask You through the Holy Spirit to come into my life and make Jesus not just my Savior but the Lord of my life from this day forward. Amen.*

Please find a Bible-teaching church that lives out the walk of faith. This is important that you might be ministered to and continue to grow. In the act of committing your life to Jesus by walking through His door, you have become a follower of Jesus, that is, trusting Him with your life.

Chapter 9

THE "CHOCOLATE MILK" SECRET

The secret to growing and developing your relationship with Jesus Christ

When I joined staff with Athletes in Action (AIA), I remember hearing the illustration in this chapter for the first time, and it changed my life! I do not know where it originally came from, but I have used it many, many times when speaking and sharing with individuals. In fact, for years, when I was asked to speak for the first time, I would share nothing else but this talk and illustration. It is that important!

Imagine three clear bottles full of milk. Each of these bottles represents a person's state of being that the Bible describes in 1 Corinthians 2:14–3:3.

> *"But a **natural man** does not accept the things of the Spirit of God, for they are foolishness to him; and he cannot understand them, because they are spiritually appraised. But **he who is spiritual** appraises all things, yet he himself is appraised by no one. For who has known the mind of the Lord, that he will instruct Him? But we have the mind of Christ"* (1 Corinthians 2:14–16).

#1

The first bottle (#1) is filled with plain white milk, which represents the ***natural man.*** Jesus Christ is not in this person's life (notice there is no lid on bottle #1).

#2

The second bottle of milk (#2) has a lot of chocolate syrup in it, and the lid is on and it's been shaken up. This bottle represents the changed life, he who is spiritual. Jesus Christ is in this person's life. Jesus changes us from the inside out and lives in us. This causes us to appear different to others. Can you see the change from white milk to that beautiful brown chocolate color? Can you taste that new flavor added to your life? It is a new and amazing change. This illustrates how we died to ourselves and let Him take over.

The lid being on the chocolate milk bottle represents being sealed in the Spirit, as we read in Ephesians 1:13–14: *"In Him, you also, after listening to the message of truth, the gospel of your salvation — having also believed, **you were sealed in Him with the Holy Spirit of promise,** who is given as a pledge of our inheritance, with a view to the redemption of God's own possession, to the praise of His glory."* The apostle Paul, the author, uses the word "sealed," referring to the signet seal of a king's ring. This seal would be placed on a letter, a declaration with the utmost importance from the king. If someone broke the seal, it was punishable by death. What a picture! We are sealed by God with His Spirit through the blood of Christ (that's why He had to die). We are sealed by this King, God.

Now consider bottle #3. Have you ever made a glass of chocolate milk, forgot to drink it, and left it on the counter? What happens?

Bottle #3 shows all the chocolate syrup resting on the bottom with white milk on top. Notice this bottle also has a lid on it. This represents the worldly person (that is, a person controlled by the world) — one who has received Christ but there appears to be no difference from a natural person. First Corinthians 3:1–3 says, *"And I, brethren, could not speak to you as to spiritual men, but as to* **men of flesh,** *as to infants in Christ. I gave you milk*  *to drink, not solid food; for you were not yet able to receive it. Indeed, even now you are not yet able, for you are still fleshly. For since there is jealousy and strife among you, are you not fleshly,* **and are you not walking like mere men?"**

#3

A lot of people, if honest, would describe themselves as bottle #3. They would say they have asked Jesus Christ into their life (they've "said the prayer"), but their life doesn't look any different from bottle #1. That, my friend, is a great tragedy in the majority of our Christian churches and communities — we do not look any different from a person who is non-spiritual. OUCH! (That was me, too.)

#2 ⇨ #3

So the question that needs to be asked is, What happens to cause us to go from bottle #2 to bottle #3?

The answer, spelled out, is **S** – **I** (super loud) – **N**. That's right ... sin. Did you get the emphasis on **"I"** when I spelled it out for you? **I** is for independence, and that's what sin is; the moment we become independent from God, we sin. How many times a day are we independent from God?

Let's consider what pleases God: living by faith, trusting Him, believing in Him, our dependence on Him. This is when He draws near to us. So what is the opposite of dependence? It is when we are independent of Him. This may sound subtle, but isn't that how Satan works ... in subtleties? Breaking one of the 10 Commandments is obvious sin that is gross evidence of our independence, but how often have you and I lived independently from God each and every day? When I understand that this makes me a sinner every day, it helps me to be a little bit more humble. While murder, lying, and coveting are definitely sins from the 10 Commandments, not depending on Him in faith in my daily tasks is also what I believe the Bible calls sin.

Back to our chocolate milk illustration. Let's look at three verses that explain what happens to the Spirit within us when we sin:

1. Ephesians 4:30 – *"Do not grieve the Holy Spirit of God, by whom you were sealed for the day of redemption."*

Sin grieves the Spirit within us. This is an emotional grieving. I have a nephew, Josh, who when he was a toddler would start crying because his spirit was crushed. He could hardly talk or breathe and would start turning blue; we would have to remind him to breathe by saying, "Josh, breathe." Having that emotion in mind is like when God says to Noah in Genesis 6:7, *"I will blot out man whom I have created from the face of the land, from man to animals to creeping things and to birds of the sky; **for I am sorry that I have made them.**"*

2. 1 Thessalonians 5:19 – *"Do not quench the Spirit"*

Furthermore, sin quenches the Spirit that lives within us, like throwing water on a fire or a burning stick into water. Can you hear it being quenched? That is what we do to the Spirit when we live independently from God.

3. Hebrews 10:29 – *"How much severer punishment do you think he will deserve who has trampled under foot the Son of God, and has regarded as unclean the blood of the covenant by which he was sanctified, and has insulted the Spirit of grace?"*

#3

Finally, did you know that according to the Book of Hebrews, we insult the Holy Spirit when we are independent of Him? We are an insult to the Spirit.

These three verses help explain bottle #3 to us.

Following Christ Through the Spirit-Filled Life

Ephesians 5:18 says, *"And do not get drunk with wine, for that is dissipation, but be filled with the Spirit."* Being filled with the Spirit is the secret to the abundant life that Jesus promises us in John 10:10 when He says, *"I came that they may have life, and have it abundantly."* As Jesus says in the same verse in the same breath, *"The thief comes only to steal and kill and destroy."* When we are living a life as exemplified in bottle #3, this is exactly what the enemy has done. Do not get ripped off, as so many are.

Let's go to the text of Ephesians 5:15–18 to learn the key to staying full in Christ. I have used a study method to make it easier to understand. Notice the three "not/but" contrasting statements that are underlined.

> *15 Therefore be careful how you walk,*
>   <u>not</u> *as* **unwise** *men*
>   <u>but</u> *as wise,*   contrast #1
>   *16making the most of your time,*
>   *because the days are evil.*
> *17 So then do* <u>not</u> *be* **foolish,**
>   <u>but</u> *understand what the will of the Lord is.*   contrast #2
> *18 And do* <u>not</u> *get drunk with wine,*
>   *for that is* **dissipation,**
>   <u>but</u> *be filled with the Spirit*   contrast #3

Also notice the negative progression of *unwise, foolish,* and *dissipation.* Dissipation is a strong word that means "to fully waste." The contrast is clear between the unwise and the wise. The key, the secret to walking with Christ, is to **"be filled with the Spirit."**

After becoming a Christ-follower, this is the greatest truth to living a successful life unto Jesus. As my wife has described it in her own words, "The understanding of this truth got me off the rollercoaster ride of ups and downs." It is honestly what has set me free, too. The Spirit-filled life empowers us to follow Christ.

The big question is, How do we get from being bottle #3 back to being bottle #2, "filled"?

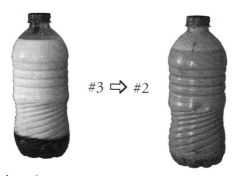

#3 ⇨ #2

Let's explore how a person is filled with the Holy Spirit. In Acts 2:33, the Holy Spirit is what the Father promised to the followers of Jesus Christ: *"Therefore having been exalted to the right hand of God, and having received **from the Father the promise of the Holy Spirit,** He has poured forth this which you both see and hear."* At this moment in history, known as Pentecost, the disciples were given the Holy Spirit. Today, the Holy Spirit comes into a person's life the moment he or she chooses to follow Christ. That choice to follow Jesus is because of the Holy Spirit's work of opening a person's eyes to Christ and regenerating him or her. It is all due to the Holy Spirit's work in someone's life.

In Ephesians 5:18, Paul contrasts being filled with the Spirit to getting drunk with wine. Have you seen someone empowered by alcohol, in a drunken state? You probably have, as I have too many times. Some get bold when drunk, empowered to do things they wouldn't normally do. A drunk would need to continue to drink and drink to stay drunk. In the same way, as Christ-followers, we are to be filled with the Holy Spirit, boldly empowered by Him.

Paul is commanding that we are to be filled with the Spirit.

The verb used here is one of the most unique in Scripture: *"be filled."* It is imperative, plural, passive, and present tense.

Imperative means this is a command of God, not up for debate, not a suggestion. This is also true when, in the same verse, Paul says not to get drunk.

Plural shows that the command is for every believer.

Passive means it was done one time and one time only. When you become a Christ-follower, the Holy Spirit comes in and dwells in you. It is not about us possessing more of the Spirit, but allowing the Spirit to possess more of us. A great question to ask yourself is, "Does the Holy Spirit have me?"

Present means it is ongoing. We are responsible to keep being filled with the Spirit daily, better said, moment by moment throughout each and every day. This continual filling is not a one-time event. Don't confuse this with the one-time indwelling of the Spirit at the moment of salvation. We are to yield to the Spirit's filling because it is an ongoing need for followers of Jesus. We need to be fully open to Him, all the time, an ongoing availability.

When we sin and look like bottle #3, we first need to confess our sin. First John 1:9 says, *"If we confess our sins, He is faithful and righteous to forgive us our sins and to cleanse us from all unrighteousness."* If you believe that He already forgave you of your sins, past, present, and future, that is true; otherwise, Jesus would need to die on the cross again.

Please understand this truth: Once the relationship between God and you (His child) is established, it can never be broken. What does happen is that *fellowship* between you and God is broken when you sin or live independently of Him. It's just like when you are in a relationship with another person. You can feel when the fellowship gets broken, right? And what do you need to do to mend the relationship? Confess what you have done wrong and ask for forgiveness. If you are married, you know that means over and over again. In marriage, you are still in a married relationship, but the fellowship can and does get broken.

When my children do something wrong, I want them to acknowledge it, ask for forgiveness, and repent from doing it again. "Confess" is a military term that means acknowledging what you have done. If the act was done in public, acknowledge it publicly, too. If it was in private or in thought, then confess in private. I would encourage you to say your confession out loud to God; there is something powerful when you verbally say it and hear your own confession to God.

We need to ask God to fill us back up with the Holy Spirit. First John 5:14–15 says, *"This is the confidence which we have before Him, that, **if we ask anything according to His will**, He hears us. And if we know that He hears us in whatever we ask, we know that we have the requests which we have asked from Him."* This is how you get "yes" answers to your prayers. Is it God's will that we are filled with His Spirit? We know that it is a command and He is faithful to His Word. When we ask, we need to trust, by faith, that He will fill us. Therefore, it will be done. It is not a feeling.

I suggest walking through these two steps:

First, ask God where you have broken fellowship with Him. I would like you to sit quietly somewhere with a piece of paper and start writing down those things that come to mind. Warning: you might write down more than you first intended to. Write as God shows you. That is your confession to the Lord. Then, do what God does with it ... He removes our sins and has compassion on us!

Psalm 103:12 says, *"As far as the **east** is from the **west,** so far has He **removed** our transgressions from us."* Have you ever wondered why God did not use north and south? It is because there are two poles, and that means they are measurable. On the other hand, when you go east and west, you can go forever either way. Wow!

Micah 7:19 says, *"He will again have compassion on us; He will tread our iniquities under foot. Yes, You **will cast all their sins into the depths of the sea."*** This is a beautiful picture. The problem comes when we start dredging our sins up again. We must trust the Word of God. He does not want us beating ourselves up once we have confessed to Him. So many people, like me, will martyr themselves. I think of it like this: If a dog represents sin and it bites us in the leg, instead of getting rid of the dog, we break out the saw and cut off our leg. Do not do that. Once you have confessed, you are forgiven because of Jesus' blood shed on the cross.

Second, ask God to fill you back up with His Spirit by faith, and He will do so. If you try to live the Christian life in your own power, you will feel frustrated and ultimately will fail. You must be dependent on God for His help, and that's why He gave each one of us the Holy Spirit to live within us. The key is to do this moment by moment, not just at church, but as soon as you realize you've

#2

sinned. This practice is something you may have to do multiple times in one day to stay filled with the Spirit. Do not get discouraged! Keep practicing this biblical truth so you can live the abundant life, the "chocolate milk life."

Chapter 10

A TROPHY OF GRACE

Do you see yourself as God's trophy of grace?

When my wife, Alison, and I were ministering to college athletes at the University of Hawai'i for more than a decade, I was blessed to be part of the chaplaincy team for the Pro Bowl (NFL All-Star game) every year. At first I was enamored with the stars of the NFL with whom I was blessed to have conversations, but that quickly changed. I was asked by many people, "What is it like to work with them?" I would answer that many of the men were still trying to find their identity. A few guys felt so unworthy to be there that they even contemplated suicide. These men, who were worshiped by many, still needed to look in the mirror and try to figure out who they really were.

Think about all the things that have motivated you in the past during your athletic journey. For me these things have been recognition, anger, protecting my teammates, and sometimes even winning at all costs. I left God in the locker room too many times as I went out and competed at practice or in a game.

I would like to share two related vignettes that illustrate how I had no clue how to worship the Lord while competing and, instead, to find my self-worth, I was attempting to position myself among my peers in the high school sports world as a player with a horrible image and appalling reputation.

Once in a non-league football game, things got ugly. I was playing defensive end, and when the opposing tight end came out of the huddle and got into his stance, I was looking at his hand to read what he might be doing. I noticed that his fingernails were all extraordinarily long. Then I noticed that scratched into his helmet was the word "Psycho." Weird! On the snap of the ball, he came to block me, as he should, but instead of using a normal blocking technique, he stepped toward me and, like an eagle stretching out its talons to grab its prey, he raked my neck with both hands. His scratching me caused my neck to bleed. My teammates asked what the heck had happened. I told them that "Psycho" had scratched me. I did not feel much until a play or two later when sweat started dripping down, and then those scratches stung. To say the least, I had my own battle going on with Psycho. In this game with Bell Jefferson High School, the tension escalated.

Then later in that game, an ugly unsportsmanlike play happened, and a bench-clearing brawl started. Immediately I looked for Psycho. He saw me and started running away. So I reacted with the dumbest thing ever; I took off my helmet, and with my strong throwing arm I fired my helmet at him, about 35 yards away. It bounced just past him. I turned and saw one of their big linemen lying on the ground. Our big lineman walked over to the guy and reached out a hand to help this opposing player up. As he reached out his hand in friendship, this guy looked up and just kicked him in the nuts, doubling my teammate over in pain. I went to help my teammate and saw Psycho coming back closer to the fight. We made eye contact and he ran off. Then all of a sudden I saw a big shadow engulf my own from behind. It was my dad. He grabbed me under the armpits, lifted me off the ground, and said, "Son, whatever you do, do not go into a football fight without your helmet on. Now go get it and get back in there!" Thanks, Dad.

A few months later, my school played a basketball game against that same high school. In truth, I had a reputation with referees, not a good one. So a large man was sent out to referee our game, obviously an ex-collegiate player. As I stepped toward the free-throw line to take shots in our pregame warmups, this referee walked out from under the basket and put his finger into my chest. With all my teammates around the key watching, I said, "What are you doing?" He said, "Look, son, you have the worst reputation with the referees in the Valley, and I want you to know they sent me to this game because of you. Now let's have a good night. I do not want any crap from you."

Because of this man's stature and deep voice, I heeded his words with reverence. I really wanted to play differently because deep down, I did not want that reputation. The game was going well, and I was controlling my mouth and temper. Then coach told us to get out and run. So I planned to grab the rebound and get the ball out to our guard as quickly as possible. The rebound was up high. I grabbed it, but instead of hitting the ground to pivot and make the pass, I turned in the air to pass to my guard, as always leading my outlet pass with my elbow. Unfortunately, I caught one of their players, probably the nicest one, square on the nose and cheek, breaking them. I went by the referee who had talked to me and said, "That was not intentional at all." He said, "I know, Mike; go to your bench," as they cared for the young man I had just hurt.

After halftime, the opposing fans were barking words to me as we warmed back up. Those things fueled me. As I went to jump center, I saw the referee go toward the other team's point guard, who had abruptly walked onto the court late with a towel. He stopped the player, took the towel, and showed his coach a foot-long steel pipe that was concealed under the towel. Their coach did not take him out. When I jumped center, someone took a swing at me. Even so, I did not retaliate because I had already hurt their teammate, and I wanted to show the referee respect. I was shocked, too.

After the game, I was walking out to the parking lot with a girl I liked at the time, named Karen. A guy from the opposing school's football team came at me with a knife in hand, threatening me. I backed up, but one of my teammates blindsided this guy with a right haymaker. I just walked on to Karen's car. Then suddenly, the girlfriend of one of these guys was swinging a five-pound mallet at me, chasing me around cars. I was not going to hit a girl, but I will confess I was more scared of her than any of the guys. She was that scary looking. What an unbelievable game night! To top it off, these were two religious-based schools, too. After that, the two schools were not allowed to play each other for four years in any sport.

If only I knew then the things I am about to share with you now.

Romans 12:2 (PHILLIPS) says, *"Don't let the world around you squeeze you into its own mold, but let God remold your minds from within, so that you may prove in practice that the plan of God for you is good, meets all his demands and moves you toward the goal of true maturity."*

God's plan to give us self-worth is through Christ's finished work on the cross. In His Word, God states certain truths about a person who has chosen to accept this work of Christ, even if we don't feel like they are true. These are called "positional truths." First, however, let's look at what is true of us **before** knowing Jesus Christ as our personal Lord and Savior. These can be shocking the first time we hear these verses.

We were:

- Alienated from God (Colossians 1:21)
- Strangers to God (Ephesians 2:12, 19)
- Enemies of God (Romans 5:10)
- Unable to do good (Ecclesiastes 7:20)
- Dead in our sins (Ephesians 2:1, 2)
- Destined to the pit of hell (Psalm 40:2)
- Living in the lust of the flesh and mind (Ephesians 2:2, 3)

Furthermore, our good works were like filthy garments to God (Isaiah 64:6). These filthy garments or rags are a reference to a menstrual rag or a cloth that wrapped around a leper's open wounds. Either one is disgusting. In the same way, our good works are polluted by our selfish motives. That is how God sees our good works apart from Him.

There are two ways in which we humans beings struggle with performance:

1. We struggle with pressure to perform so we can win the **praise** and **applause** of others.

2. We struggle with pressure to perform so we will be **accepted** and **loved** by others.

In reality, what we really are seeking is SELF-WORTH!

So, how does God view our performance **after** we have surrendered our life to Christ? Let's look at five of the many positional truths about us in the Word of God:

1. Adoption

Ephesians 1:5 (KJV) says, *"Having predestined us into the adoption of children by Jesus Christ to himself, according to the good pleasure of His will."*

When a person is placed into a family after being adopted, he or she joins that new family with no financial debt and becomes an heir of his or her new parents. In some states, even, the adopted cannot ever be removed from the family inheritance, yet biologicals can be removed. In the same way, when we are adopted into Christ's family, we are given a clean slate.

2. Redemption

Ephesians 1:7 says, *"In Him we have redemption through His blood, the forgiveness of our trespasses, according to the riches of His grace."*

Think of this as like redeeming a coupon. This is, in fact, the greatest exchange ever in history: Jesus' blood for our sins. We have been freed from the slavery of sin and now live from a place of victory as followers of Jesus Christ.

In addition, Galatians 3:13a (TLB) says, *"But Christ has bought us out from under the doom of that impossible system by taking the curse for our wrongdoing upon himself."*

The "doom" refers to God's wrath that is due to each one of us.

3. Reconciled

Colossians 1:21–22 (TLB) says, *"This includes you who were once so far away from God. You were his enemies and hated him and were separated from him by your evil thoughts and actions, yet now he has brought you back as his friends. He has done this through the death on the cross of his own human body, and now as a result Christ has brought you into the very presence of God, and you are standing there before him with nothing left against you— nothing left that he could even chide [blame] you for."*

One way to understand this in reverse is to think, sadly, of how many couples go to the altar in love but then over the years they "fall out of love," and end up in court claiming irreconcilable differences. They get divorced because they cannot stand to be near each other anymore. With God we were born separated from Him. Scripture says we were enemies, but after we receive His Son's sacrifice of blood on the cross, which reconciles us to Him, He has made us His children.

4. Propitiation

First John 4:9–10 (TLB) says, *"God showed how much he loved us by sending his only Son into this wicked world to bring to us eternal life through his death. In this act we see what real love is: it is not our love for God but his love for us when he sent his Son to satisfy [or propitiate] God's anger against our sins."*

This word "propitiation" could be considered an accounting term, a balancing of the books. We deserve the wrath of God,

yet because of Jesus' sacrifice on the cross and the shedding of
His blood, God's wrath is satisfied and His love demonstrated.
This is grace!

5. Justification

Romans 5:1 (TLB) says, *"So now, since we have been made
right [justified] in God's sight by faith in his promises, we can have
real peace with him because of what Jesus Christ our Lord has done
for us."*

"Justified" is a legal term. We are being justified before the
Judge; there is no jury because the Judge is all-knowing. Again
we are only justified because of Christ's atonement for our sin.

Romans 8:1 says, *"Therefore there is now no condemnation for
those who are in Christ Jesus."* If you are a committed follower of
Jesus, justified means "just as if I never did anything wrong or
just as if I have always done everything right." This is how we
are viewed by the Father because of Christ's work on the cross.

Like I already said, these are positional truths as we place
our faith in Jesus as our Lord and Savior. Even though we do
not *feel* this way a lot of the time, they are His truth for and
about us.

The choice we face moment by moment is between these
two options, God's way or the world's way:

GOD'S WAY: Person's worth = What God says is
true about you

WORLD'S WAY: Person's worth = Performance + others'
opinions

The practical effect of our performance **before** and **after** Christ is that it takes away our PRIDE. To see who we were before Christ and to see who we are after Christ clearly shows that we did NOTHING to get from Point A to Point B!

Read these truths from God's Word:

- Psalm 40:2–3 (NIV): *"He lifted me out of the slimy pit, out of the mud and mire; he set my feet on a rock and gave me a firm place to stand. He put a new song in my mouth, a hymn of praise to our God. Many will see and fear the LORD and put their trust in him."*

- Galatians 6:3: *"If anyone thinks he is something when he is nothing, he deceives himself."*

- Philippians 3:3: *"…put no confidence in the flesh."*

When we consider what Christ has done for us, it gives us proper motivation to live out what God says is true of us in Christ.

Ephesians 1:18 (NIV) says, *"I pray that the eyes of your heart may be enlightened in order that you may know the hope to which he has called you, the riches of his glorious inheritance in his holy people."* This is a great prayer for people you love who do not know Christ because, as 2 Corinthians 4:4 tells us, their minds have been blinded by the enemy.

Again, these are only five of the many positional truths that are found in the Bible. We must spend time in God's Word daily so that we can know and live out these truths. When you choose to believe them, living by faith, then you can see yourself as a Trophy of Grace.

FINAL THOUGHTS FROM THE AUTHOR

Truly, I am a miraculous mess. The truth is that this book shares only the tip of the iceberg in my life of wounds that the Lord has healed. The things I describe in this book are the easier things to talk about. As the Lord continues to melt my heart, so much more has surfaced, yet He continues to bring healing in my life as things are brought into the light of Jesus. Praise God the iceberg in my life is shrinking rapidly. I pray yours will, too.

I would also like to share with you an important lesson that may convey why I went through what I have gone through in my life. I have been reminded of the story of Abraham and his only begotten son, Isaac. Remember when God asked Abraham to sacrifice Isaac, and Abraham was willing to do so, trusting the Lord? That sacrifice and trust are exactly what I was unwilling to do with the sports that I loved so much. I was not willing to take them before the altar of the Lord. It was all self-centered and self-serving on my part.

As I was going through my trials, my friends often called me Job. Do you remember Job's story?

The LORD said to Satan, "Have you considered My servant Job? For there is no one like him on the earth, a blame-

less and upright man, fearing God and turning away from evil." Then Satan answered the LORD, *"Does Job fear God for nothing? Have You not made a hedge about him and his house and all that he has, on every side? You have blessed the work of his hands, and his possessions have increased in the land. But put forth Your hand now and touch all that he has; he will surely curse You to Your face." Then the* LORD *said to Satan, "Behold, all that he has is in your power, only do not put forth your hand on him." So Satan departed from the presence of the* LORD (Job 1:8–12).

Job lost everything by Satan's hand — his wife, his sons and daughters, and his possessions. Job never ended up cursing the Lord but instead stayed faithful, and God blessed Job for his faithfulness by giving him everything back, even doubling his possessions. I often think that he still lost his children and wife; then it hit me that Job will have them for eternity.

So may I share with you what the Lord has given back to me? I want to boast here, that is, to boast in the Lord and what He has allowed me to do, for which I am so deeply thankful:

FOOTBALL – I never played football again, but I was blessed to coach at Grossmont High School during my later college years. Right afterward came the 1987 NFL strike. One of the coaches with whom I coached at the high school was an ex-NFL punter, having played with the Dallas Cowboys. He told me I was better as a punter than he ever had been and that he could help me get a tryout with the San Diego Chargers. However, because I was falling in love with the greatest gift of my life, I passed on his generous offer. That was a good decision because I ended up marrying this gift, Alison.

My wife and I joined Athletes in Action staff a year after being married. God allowed us to be placed at the University of Hawai'i, and I was so blessed to serve as the university's football chaplain from 1992–2003. During those years, the NFL chaplains who came to serve at the Pro Bowl invited my wife and me to serve with them.

From 2008 to 2017, I was overwhelmed by the Lord's generosity when He allowed me to serve as the UCLA Bruins football chaplain. During my first time walking down the tunnel with the football team to the field, my eyes welled up with gratitude. I felt like my childhood dream had come full circle. During this season, I was able to share a chapter of my life together with so many great men. My last game on the Rose Bowl field was UCLA versus Hawai'i. The Hawai'i football staff included five of my UH players from the time I served as their chaplain, now coaching. What a special memory!

In addition, I also got to share this sport with my son Chris, through his high school days playing for Trinity Classical Academy. In 2009 I was the offensive coordinator and special teams coach. We went 0–9 with only freshmen and sophomores in the high school. The 2011 year I was asked to be the head coach, and in just four years as a varsity program, Trinity Classical became CIF champs, shutting out the team, 46–0, that had won CIF almost every year for about seven years. Our team was a great group of players and coaches to share this with, and I was blessed to be named one of the CIF football coaches of the year. My coaching staff and players helped me receive that honor.

In 2017 I was elated to serve as a coach in the first American football Bowl game in China. There were 36 players from the

USA that we split in half and then picked the rest from the Chinese young men who played for their colleges. Truthfully, we had a great time coaching the Chinese football players and had a blast playing.

In 2018 I was also on the coaching staff with the USA football team that played in the World University championships in China. We lost to Mexico, but ended with silver. From the previous year I got reacquainted with many of the Chinese young men we had coached the year before.

BASKETBALL – After my "You're the Potter and I'm the clay" prayer, I never played basketball again. Even so, the Lord allowed me to serve as the University of Hawai'i chaplain for seven years. During this time, the Los Angeles Lakers trained every other year in Hawai'i, and I was blessed to have some great conversations with some of your favorite Lakers.

From 2009–2013, I was happy to serve as the assistant varsity basketball coach at Trinity Classical Academy. In the 2012–2013 season, we were in the CIF finals and received an invitation to play in the State tournament.

Furthermore, around UCLA during my time there, I was able to get to know a few of the student-athletes who played for the Bruins when they came to our weekly Bible studies.

BASEBALL – Similar to basketball, I never played the game of baseball again after my "Hurt Me Again" prayer. Later, when I was going to school at San Diego State University, I was throwing at the same time as some of the baseball players whom I knew. Head Coach Jim Dietz approached me and said some of his players had told him I was a good pitcher. He asked if I would consider coming out, but I did not have any eligibility left so I just thanked him for honoring me by even asking me to consider playing for him. Instead I took a baseball class from Coach Dietz. He gave me some great advice, which helped me get a position to coach the Granite Hills High School staff for a couple of years. There, I was surrounded with a lot of talent, including two players who would become well-known MLB players. In this opportunity, I was excited to share what I wished I would have known in high school with these high school players. These two players were Brian Giles and Shane Spencer. Brian played in two MLB All-Star games, and Shane was in four World Series with the New York Yankees.

In addition to coaching, I also was blessed to serve as the University of Hawai'i baseball chaplain for a number of years alongside Coaches Les Murakami and Mike Trapasso.

While in Hawai'i, I also served as the head chaplain for the high A minor league winter ball teams. This role was so fun because each team was made up of the best prospects from the USA, Japan, and Korea. I led the Honolulu Sharks, and all the guys who attended chapel made it to the major leagues.

In addition, I founded the Trinity Classical Academy baseball program and served as the head coach from 2010 to 2013. This role was extra special because I was blessed to coach my son Chris through his high school years. One amazing game sticks out in my memory. Chris was pitching and retired the first 19 batters in a game. The 20th batter hit a rocket just past the third baseman. Our shortstop, Dakota Prochnow, came up with the ball and gunned out the hitter to preserve the perfect game opportunity. Best play I have ever seen in my life on the baseball field! Chris lost a perfect game to the next batter on a shallow pop-up, but he struck out the 22nd batter. That was a very special night to watch him pitch.

As I write this book, I currently serve as the UCLA baseball chaplain and have enjoyed every moment of this role.

Bonus Blessings in My Life

Remember my promise to God that day I walked off the baseball field? I did become a youth pastor, which was a gift. One of my students was a young man who raced all around the place. I often had to yell at him to slow down on his bicycle: Jimmie Johnson #48 of NASCAR.

Through Athletes in Action I have been blessed to serve at a Winter Olympics in 1998; at three Summer Olympics — 1992 and 2000 with my wife, Alison, and 2016 with Alison and our three children; and at the Asian Games in 2018.

VOLLEYBALL – While dating, Alison and I played volleyball every chance we got. When we were assigned to the University of Hawai'i to start AIA there in 1991, we arrived shortly after the death of a volleyball player named Tyler Bates. This tragic event allowed me to have instant access to the men's team. I was their chaplain for a number of years. Alison worked with the women's team. I was very close with the women's head coach, Dave Shoji. Through AIA in 1994 and 2014, I got to play and coach summer volleyball tours that took me through Thailand, Japan, and Myanmar. One of my greatest joys was watching three young men grow up to become USA Olympians: Kawika and Erik Shoji and Micah Christenson. I'm so proud of them and the men they have turned into off the court.

My reader, I challenge you: Dream about what God can do with you! His dreams for you will always fit into His Great Commission to go and make disciples of all nations. Live by faith!

I would love to hear how God has used the truths in this book to impact your life. You can join our Facebook page at More Than That.

ABOUT THE AUTHOR

Mike Buchanan has been on staff with Athletes in Action since 1990. He and his wife, Alison, now serve with International Chaplaincy Acceleration Team (ICAT) developing sport chaplains. He has served as a regional director over two regions, plus spent a decade at UCLA and 12½ years at the University of Hawai'i as the campus director. Mike has ministered to coaches and athletes at all levels: professional, Olympic, college, high school, and youth. He has an A.S. from College of the Canyons, a B.S. in Physical Education (coaching) from San Diego State University, and an M.A. in Religion, *summa cum laude* from International College and Graduate School. He is committed to being a lifelong learner and to **Soli Deo gloria** (Soli Deo gloria is a Latin term for "Glory to God alone"). Mike is married to Alison (his "sunset" and gift from God), and they have three treasures from God: Christopher, Emily, and Johnny.

Made in the USA
San Bernardino, CA
08 February 2020

63877144R00066